AF580158

A CARNIVAL OF MIMICS

MAX KOZLOFF

A CARNIVAL OF MIMICS

MAX KOZLOFF

pH powerHouse Books BROOKLYN, NY

A CARNIVAL OF MIMICS

To introduce the subjects pictured in this book, I need to touch for a moment upon some human habits way back from history, in fact pre-history.

In the days of hunter-gatherers, our ancestors adopted a faith that helped to assuage the loneliness of their species. It also consoled them for the brevity of their earthly life. These humans upheld the possibility of leading an imperishable spiritual afterlife in heaven. The thought was based upon a notion that individuals possess a capacity known as a soul, a center of thought, feeling and action, entirely separable from the body but at the heart of human consciousness. Even inorganic things, composed of matter, were sometimes equipped with souls, and could participate in the continuity of our perception. This anthropomorphic fantasy, which persists in areas of our world, is called animism.

Here was a belief system that would kindle the production of would-be human life-forms, endowed with great physical longevity. In fact, many were regarded as tokens of survival beyond mortal limits, and therefore sacred in aura. This helped to affirm the idea that myths—supernatural events—could be credible in their own right, especially when used to facilitate a social order among cooperative tribes. Conceits of animistic awareness have in fact profoundly affected the subject of the human figure, as channeled in histories of art. If sculptors could conjure some imminence of soul when they materialize bodily forms, then their works could keep us company beyond the reach of neutral, useful or unconcerned artifacts. But many of the expressive, three-dimensional figures that I've photographed—and gathered here to make a point—were intended to perform more specific roles in the environment than just to keep us company. They've served to provoke desire, encourage shopping, memorialize the dead, bask in sanctity, work as ornament, recall historical deeds, compete for social status, or take us on.

For my part, I add my own credulous welcome to these far flung creations by suggesting that figures made of inorganic material could be as interactive with their own kind as are figures composed of living flesh and blood—regardless of definite evidence to the contrary. In real life and time, their scenes certainly existed as remote from, and alien to each other. Yet, there were many opportunities to show that these figures were socially engaged by seeming convergences of "behavior," or by enacting their differences of opinion about mutual issues.

To bring off this impression, I take advantage of double-page spreads in book design, which may foster persuasive yet untoward comparisons. What separated the locales of these figures in actual historical time and culture, I have compressed to only a few inches of literal margin. Symbolic as they are, many of these plaster, bronze, wax, silicone or marble figures, these effigies, dummies and mannequins, had worldly jobs to do. And carried them out with typifying costumes, gazes or gestures. Additionally, they had their designated posts or territories, which were to be respected. But when such actors were to be found elsewhere, as if gone astray with a freelance spirit, I was happy to notice their vagrancies.

Even by themselves and thousands of miles apart, I can make it appear as if these mimes might be in contact with each other. A musician who decorates a corner of a palace in Potsdam, Germany, blows a horn and billows his cheeks. On the right, a stone angel in a Mexican cemetery, cautions visitors to keep quiet and show reverence for the dead.

In 2018, during the time this book was being structured, the Metropolitan Museum of Art in New York mounted a show called "Like Life: Sculpture, Color, and the Body." It arranged shelter for many uncanny works that I would have been delighted to encounter less conveniently outdoors in more provocative settings. The museum's encouragement for visitors to study the filial course of styles and concepts in artistic idioms implies the seriousness of the content on display. Here the objects of study highlighted a tradition of illusionism that traveled way past accepted realist styles. Faces could be toned to show apparently live complexions, while real clothes, hair and jewels could be "worn": all this to instill an immediacy of contact, and the almost violent approach of the lifelike to breathing life itself. Or, to put it more directly, the hyperrealist body, nominally a figure represented, threatens to become that which was represented—in fetish or proxy form. Casts from death masks were sometimes used to enhance such illusionary effects. I wouldn't want any pieces like these to wink at me.

When they are acquired by museums, such objects are slotted in to the collection, where they are put under protective, scholarly custody. This is a dignified condition, backed up by institutional sponsorship. It also transmits any original rhetorical function of the work toward an afterlife in the form of a pedagogical lesson.

If an equestrian statue of a Confederate general is removed from a Southern plaza to a museum, the work will still speak of history, but no longer for just any proprietary cause, or a tribe's regretful nostalgia. Rather, it might share its space with other memorial objects as part of a collective, multinational legacy, however still fondly regarded by secessionist partisans of slavery. A more extreme downgrade is inferred by the gaggle of socialist realist sculptures relegated to a seedy park in a rural Budapest suburb. With Lenin most prominent, they once signified a Russian ideological dominance over Cold-War Hungary. But as values changed, and with them history, so did the honor once attributed to Soviet monumentality. At the ticket booth, one could buy a music cassette entitled "Communism's Greatest Hits." My comparisons can even show, ridiculously, that a Las Vegas hotel's entertaining imitation of an Egyptian pharaoh cannot equal the grandeur of the real thing, incarnated by the big shots at Karnak. The displacement of figures from their normal, presiding locale tells us something about the fading of their original messages, political or commercial. Their interest as objects may still remain, but their authority as power symbols had a limited shelf life. As one of my colleagues Charles Traub, said: "Propaganda is advertising we dislike."

When I depict propaganda signage or statuary, in this sense, I am not advocating or denigrating a cause; I am giving it attention through my frame and for my own purposes. Being a street photographer, I have less concern for the integrity and categories of social types than for their diffusion. Let the frame be filled with passers-by. The picture attends to their energies, manners and awareness. So much the better if that goal includes vivacious figures, deserving of the name "mimics."[1] They have apparently more readable or public roles to play than do those in mixed worldly traffics.

Mimics quite often were meant to perform at being figures of authority, like the angel. By their rank or grandeur of scale, or dominant locale, they do stand out among ordinary citizens. But I have not seen them succeed in obtaining any outright obeisance from a crowd. This is an absence of ritual that in retrospect can enhance story content. Unimpressed people get on with their sundry lives, while the theatrical mimics have literally no life at all to live. The camera doesn't know better, but the photographer does. There can be no mutual awareness implied in such reckoning, only a kind of distracted surveillance by one party of a second party. The mimics won't complain of being monitored, on their job, for the good reason that they lack volition, speech and agency. But that is also the condition of everyone suspended within the frame.

They (or rather, their appearances) are caught and immobilized in a microsecond of exposure to light. A still photograph can be an accurate record of a scene, but the image doesn't let anyone move around. More precisely, the human glance is too slow to keep up with the experience of a flourishing current of bodies, while the camera shutter operates too quickly to settle the sense of things. When this process might absorb a viewer's time, it's because the incidents in question are necessarily undetermined, ephemeral and elusive. Most likely they didn't exist before or after the image was extracted from the ripple of broader actions available as the machine was snapped. The tableau will remain in that frozen state as long as the photo survives. This puts its human subjects in a conventional paralysis, on the same historical level as statuary mimes.

We are all carrying on with whatever, but a photograph freezes the "whatever" at necessarily circumstantial and arbitrary turns of its career. Among those "turns," I was attracted to those that looked as if a person were holding a pose. People often do that when asked to sit for their portraits. They become spinmasters of self-consciousness, offering composure based on absent models. In that sense they emerge as unofficial mimes in their own right. But the showmanship of the genuine mimes is not always affable. At Sydney's Luna Park, you are invited to enter through the mouth of a giant white clown. And at a "love hotel" in Tokyo, a huge, loathsome dragon seems ready to eat arrivals. If you expect to have some thrill or bliss within these demonic places, please know that it will come with menace. This is certainly the issue in Rome's Luna Park, where a ferocious, blond, blue-eyed muscle man challenges you to a tug of war. I demurred from taking him on, for fear of losing the tug. But I could not resist the temptation to shoot as if I were about to be a player. Finally, walking through these comedic zones, I sometimes had to restrain an impulse to cry out, "Watch your back!" One example: a gigantic reptile, mouth open, in apparent pursuit of an unaware visitor at a Mysore carnival; and another: a troubled looking fashion dummy in a Ljubljana store window, who is unconcerned about a print depicting a killer samurai on his case, for no good reason. Street photographers tend to be opportunists in search of anomalies, afforded by the law of chance. No one in these pictures was threatened by real danger, but the presumption of it occasionally lurks in the atmosphere.

How about the opposite? A celebration in which a single character is drastically isolated and out of tune. In Rome's Piazza del Popolo, a massive crowd would look joyous in spirit, except for a figure who wears a skull mask. In this guise and placed central in my frame, he spoils the elated moment. The Italians had won the world soccer championship and this character chose to put it down with a funerary gesture.

I am less interested in sports then in the mimic's hyper-contrarian reference to death. Instead of the expected inference of a live consciousness, he would embody a symbol of its absence. . . in this instance by an acknowledged, even a flaunted, absence of soul. I took the picture, rattled by his inexplicable purpose, and also by the thought that it must oppose the hope that inert matter can be recharged in an after life. How about the reverse, the thought that statues—in their material state—can be the beneficiaries of imitation by humans?

That idea came to my mind on the occasion of a march to honor Nelson Mandela in New York, where I saw a citizen addressing a live Statue of Liberty, who maybe responds. By the look of this couple, they're having a perfectly natural exchange. The prototype for her get-up dates back to that famous lady in the harbor, in turn derived from earlier icons of Hellenic Greece.

Ovid's myth of Pygmalion, the sculptor who fell in love with the beautiful woman he created, flips this plot line backward. For the beautiful woman in New York is not representing a statue, she is impersonating a statue. With her living body, she publicly emulates a thing—and therefore subverts the paradigm of animism.[2] I won't say that statues need us to keep them company. But I will declare that existential issues flash through this story. In a photo that depicts the shelter of a Hare Krishna tent, visitors gaze upon a wheel of colored figures, each one the same individual, symbolic of a further stage in his aging process, until the avatar gets smaller and shrivels, like we all will, into the cycle of an end state.

1. I prefer to use the word "mimic" rather than pantomime, to indicate the sculptural presence of such figures.

2. Animism was the opposite of the effect achieved by the 18th century tradition of the tableau vivant, where famous paintings were emulated, successful if without any hint of real breathing on the part of the actual performers.

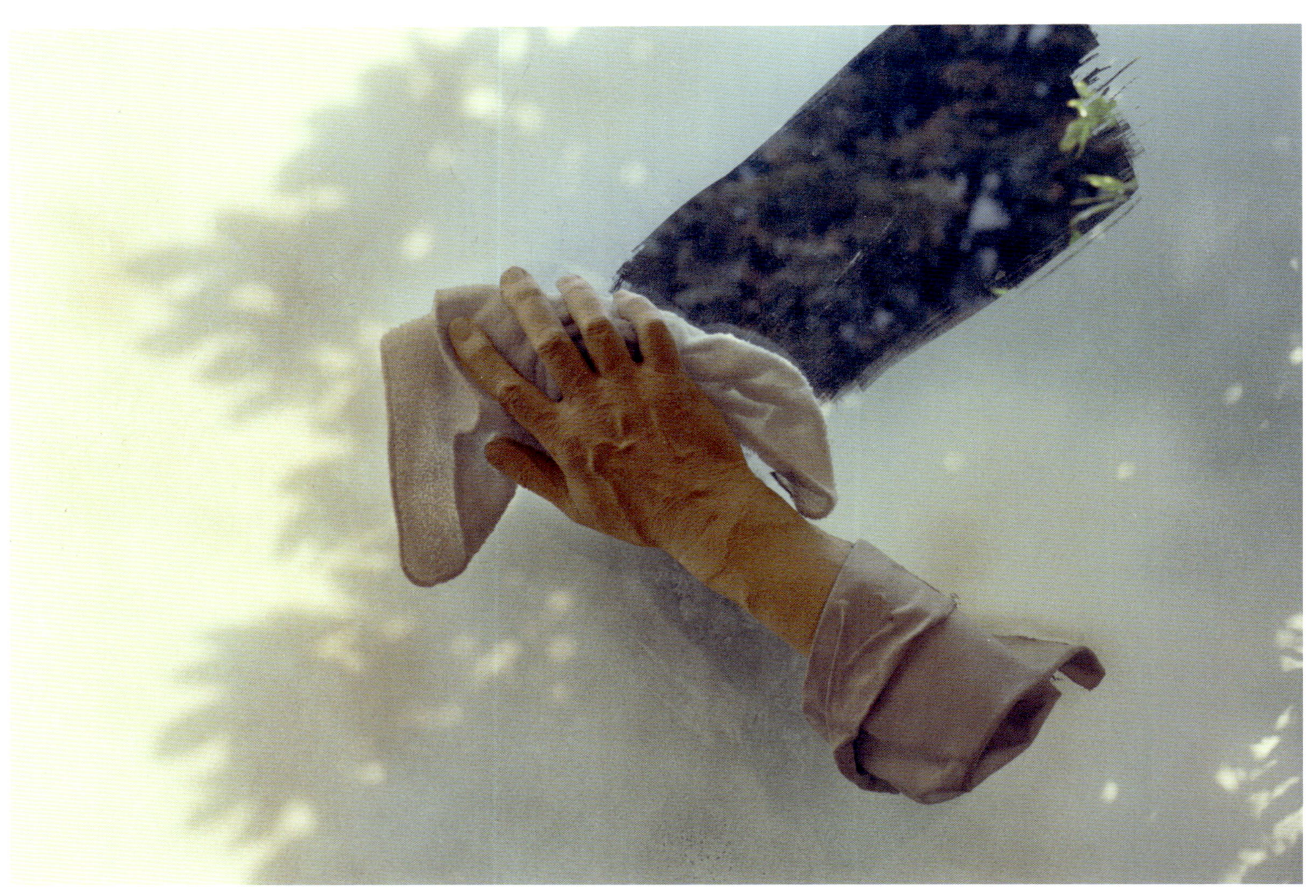

Sculptured Hand Cleaning Window, New York, 1977

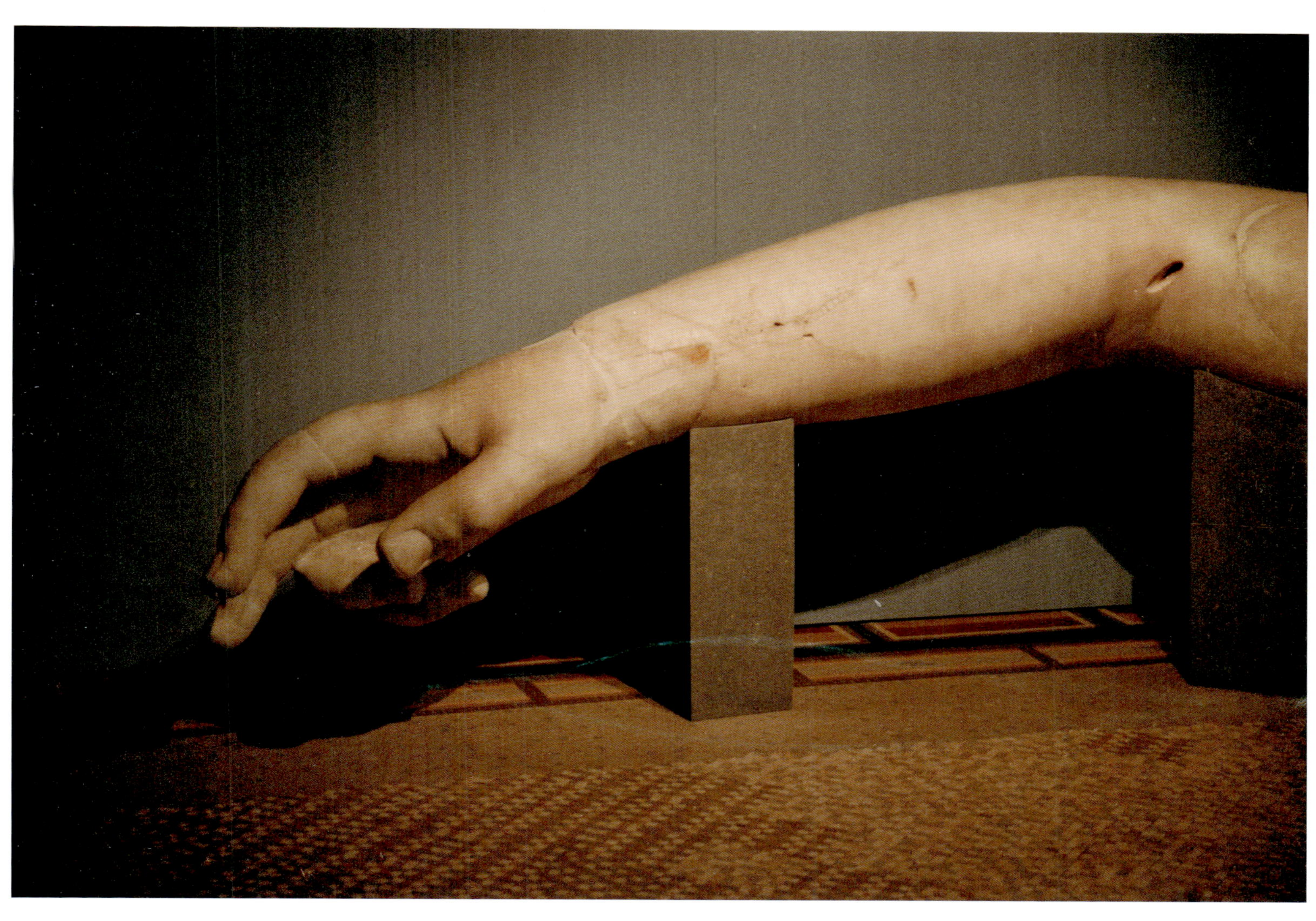

Enormous Remnant, Capitoline Museum, Rome, 1994

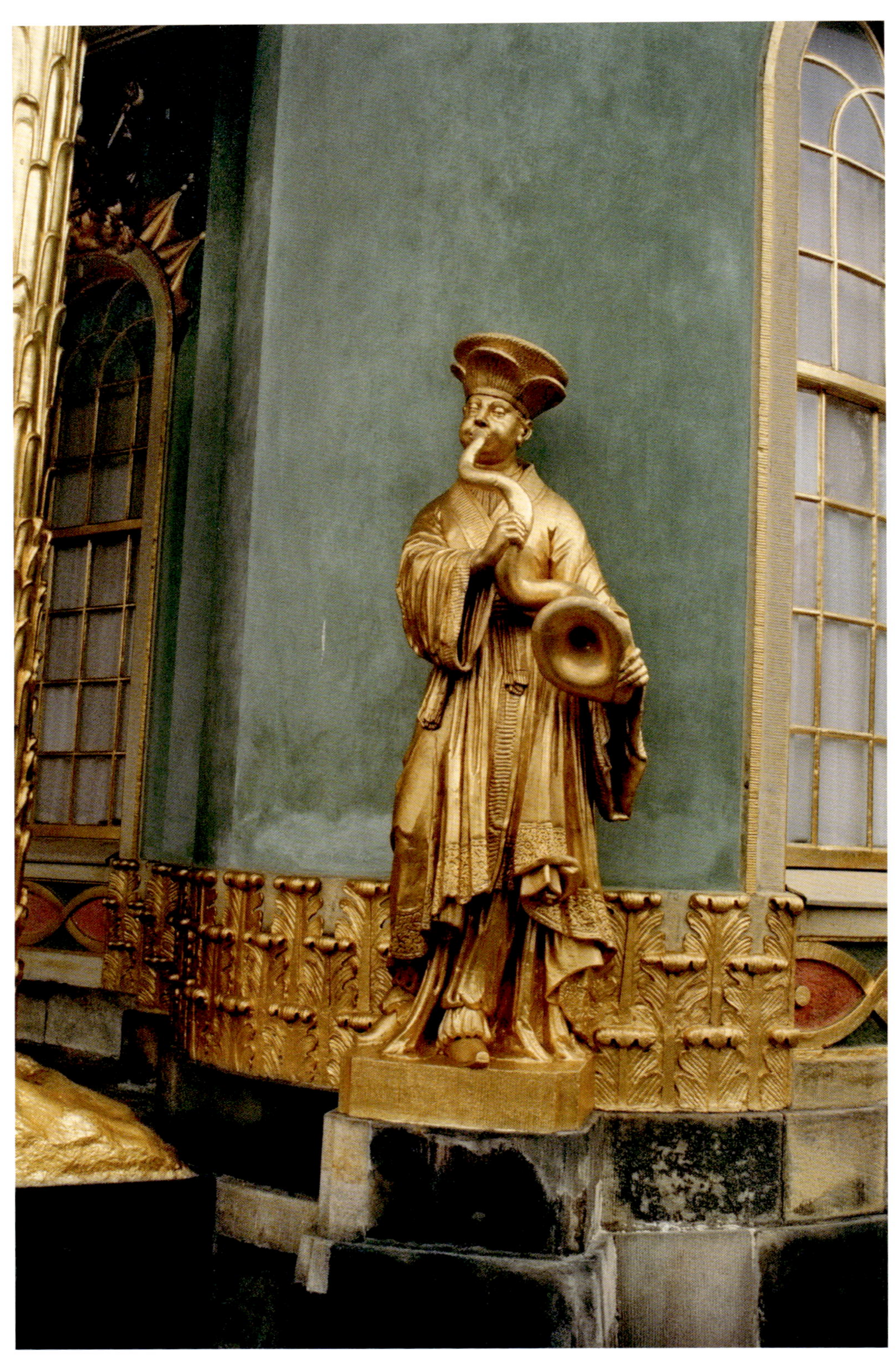

Bagpipes at Sanssouci Palace, Potsdam, 2000

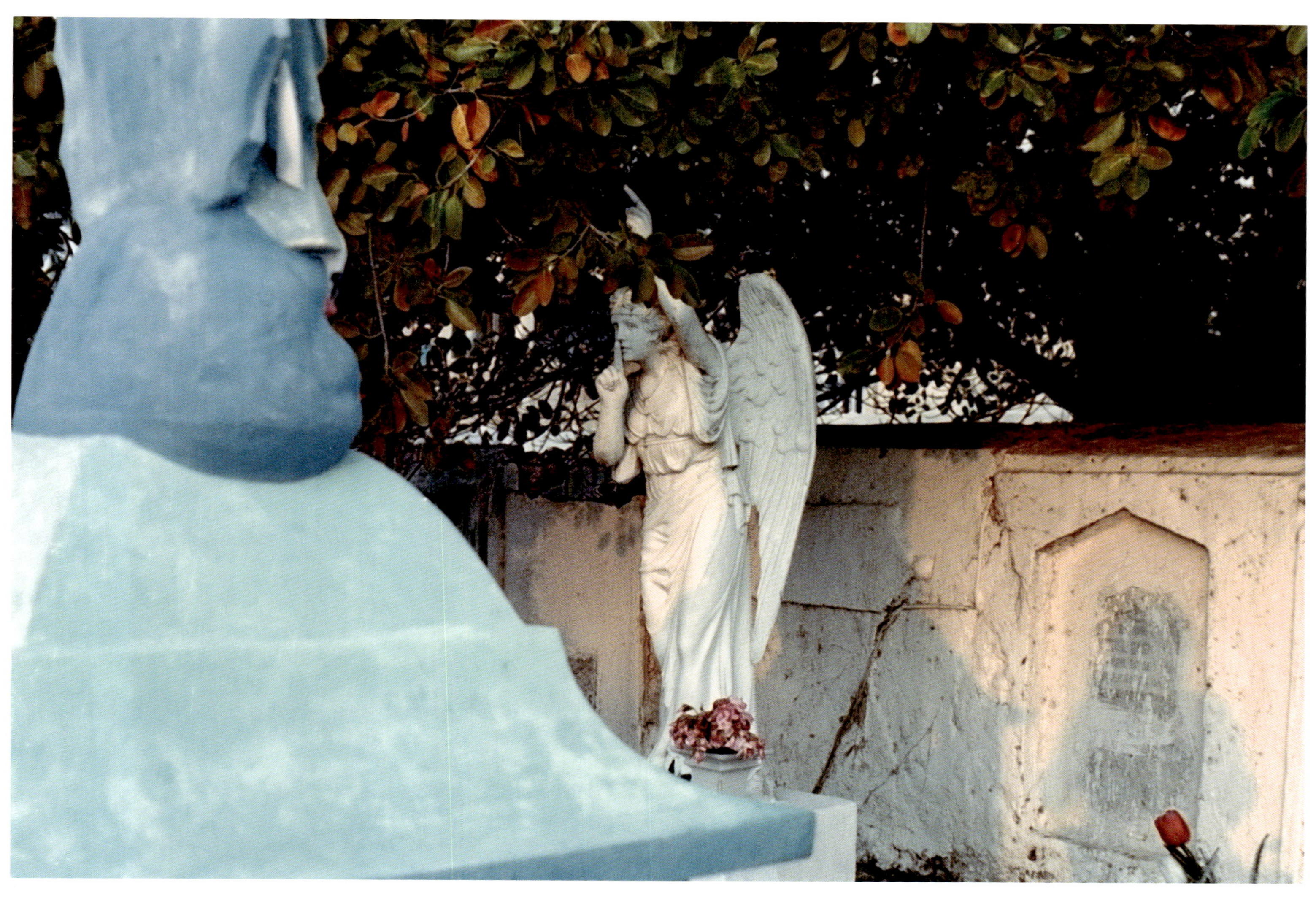

Cemetery, Isla Mujeres, Mexico, 1982

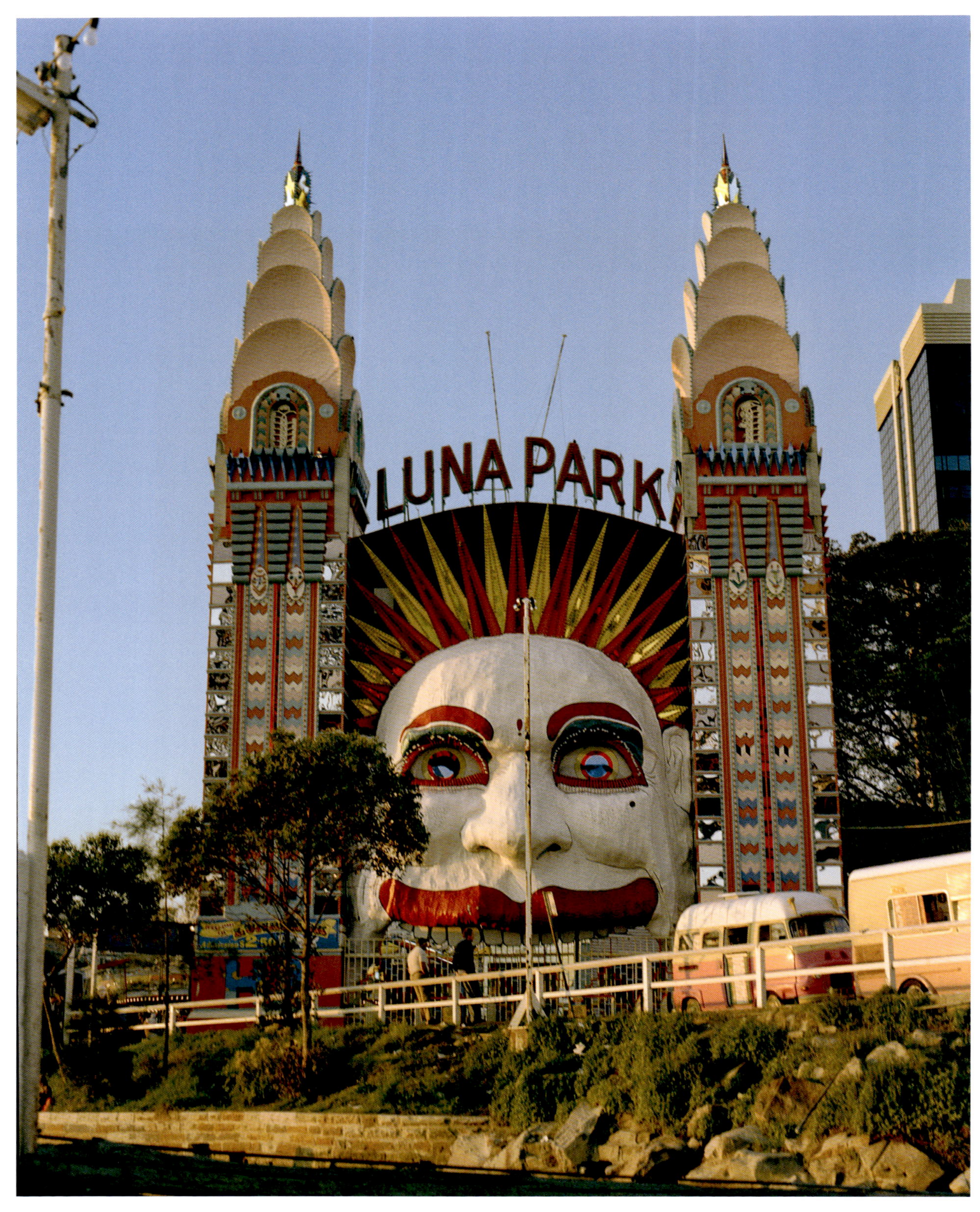

Luna Park Entrance, Sydney, 1978

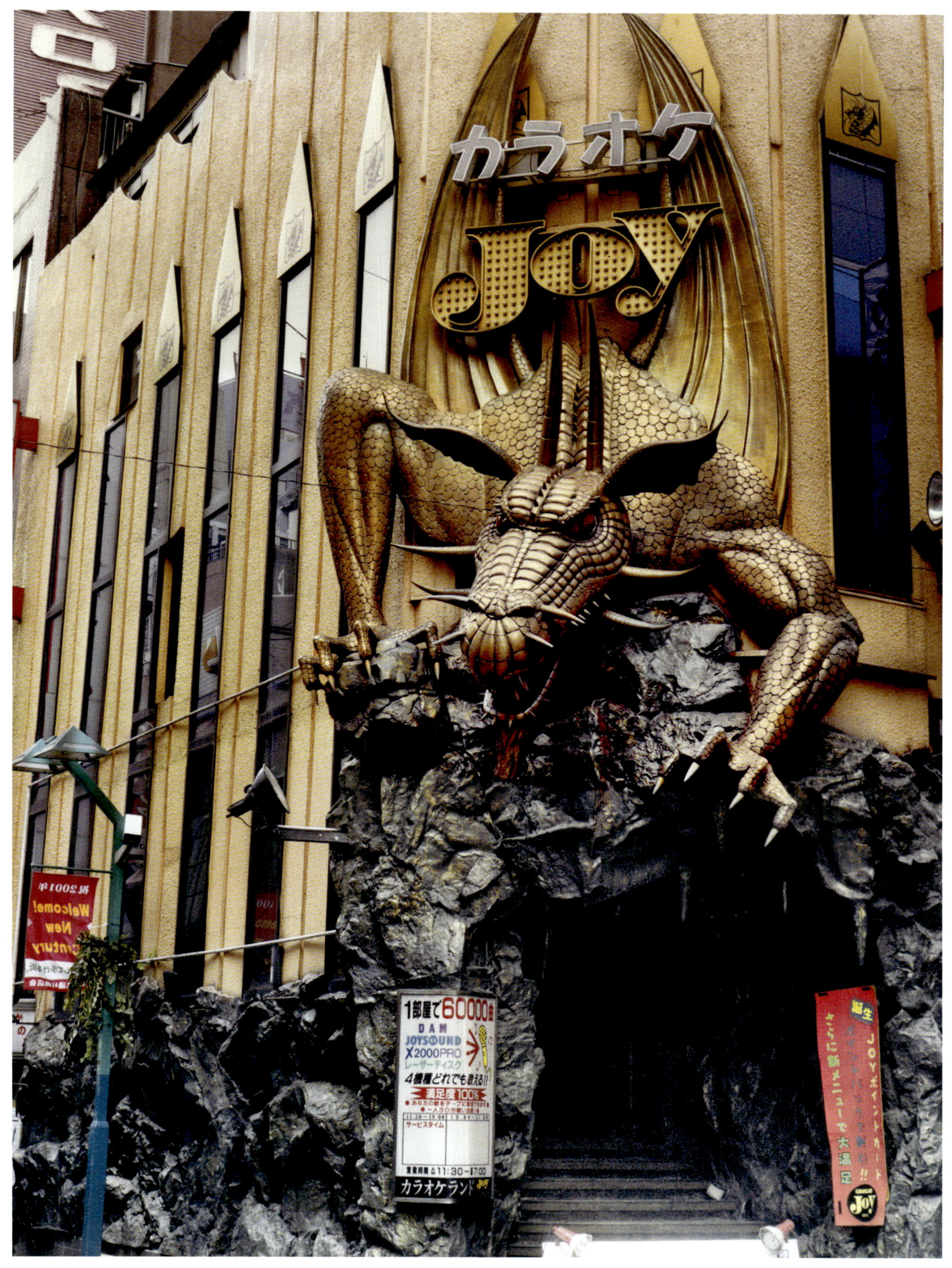

Love Hotel, Tokyo, 2001

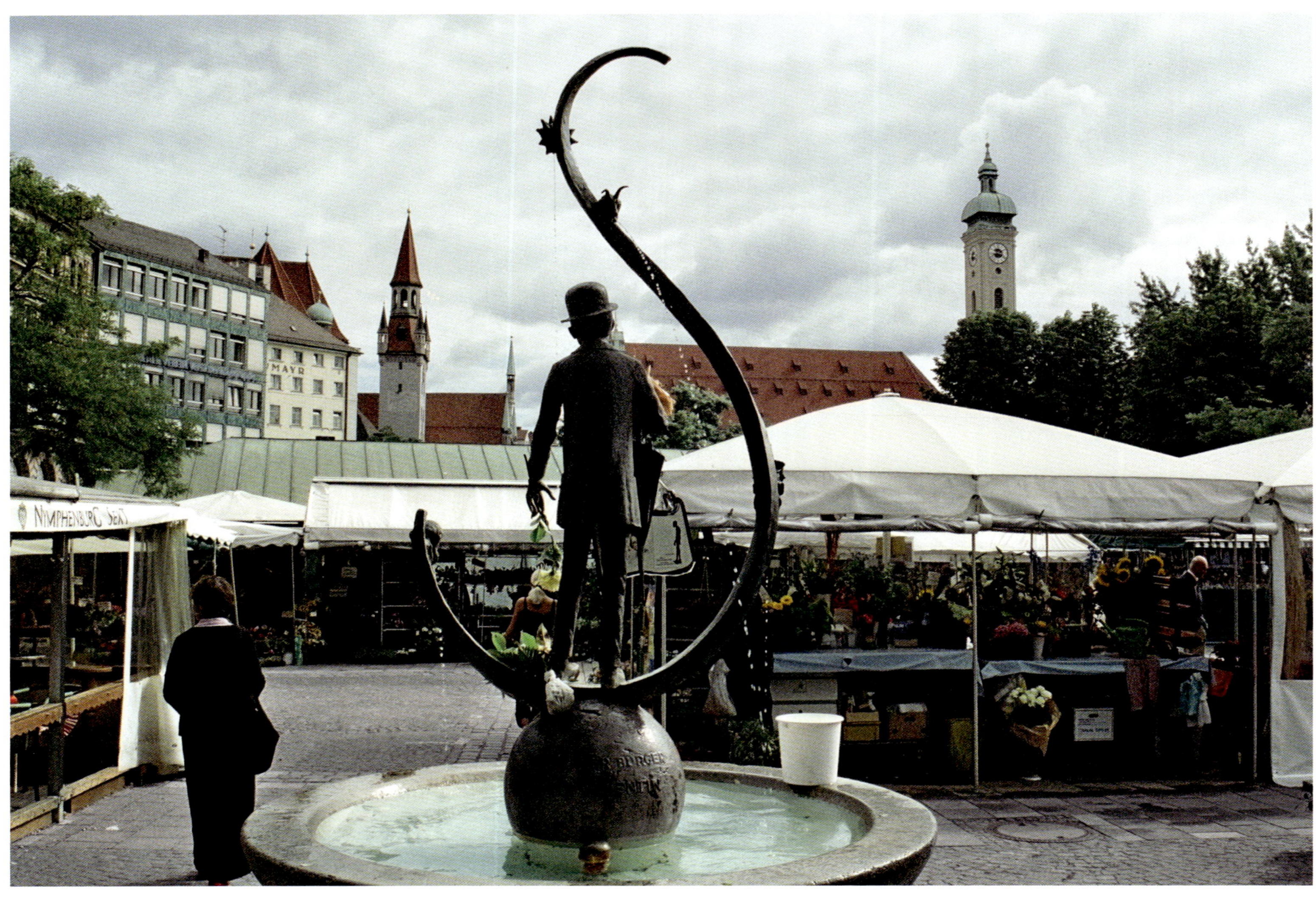

Easter Statue, Munich, 2003

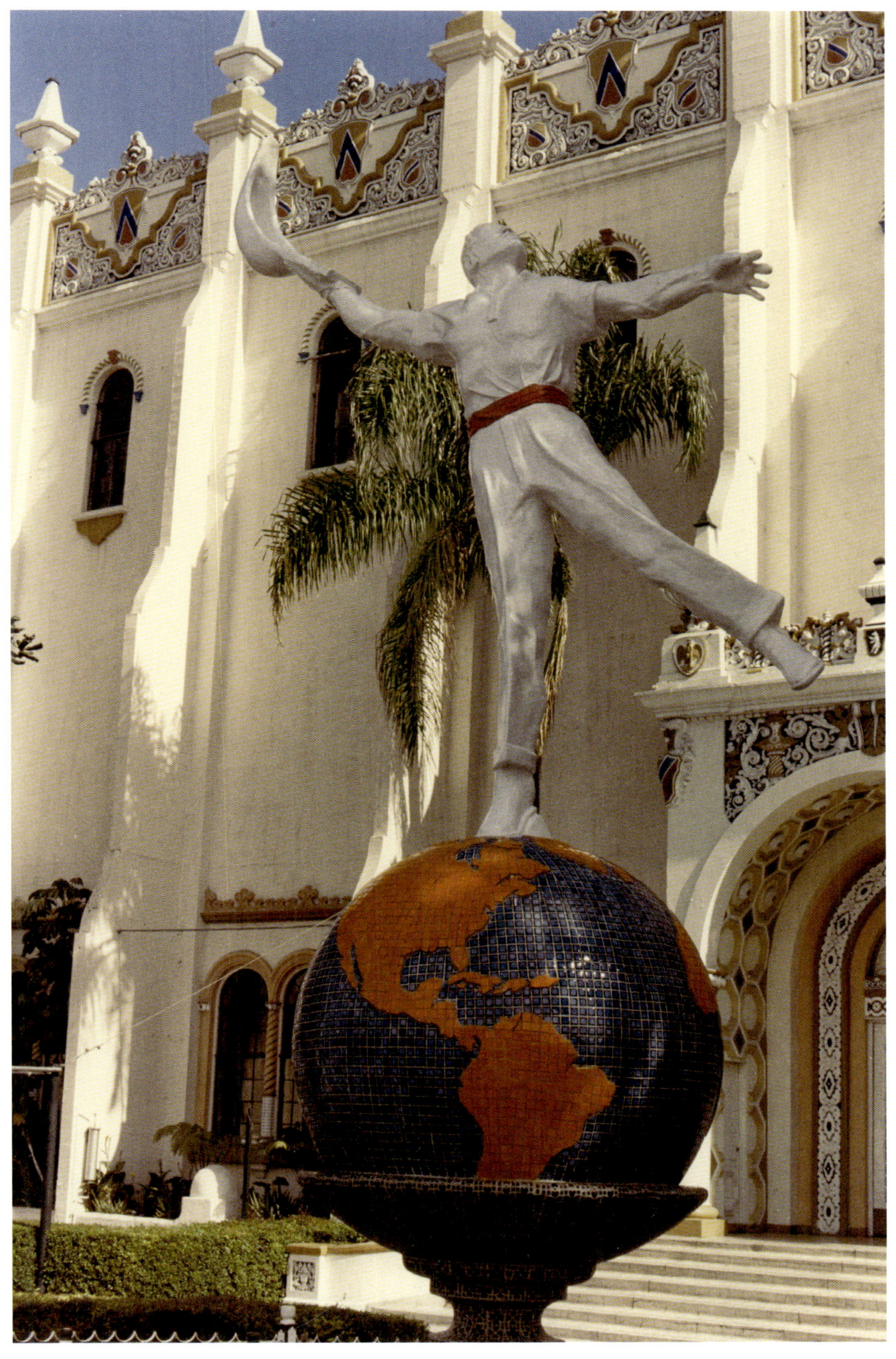

Tijuana Jai Alai, Mexico, 1998

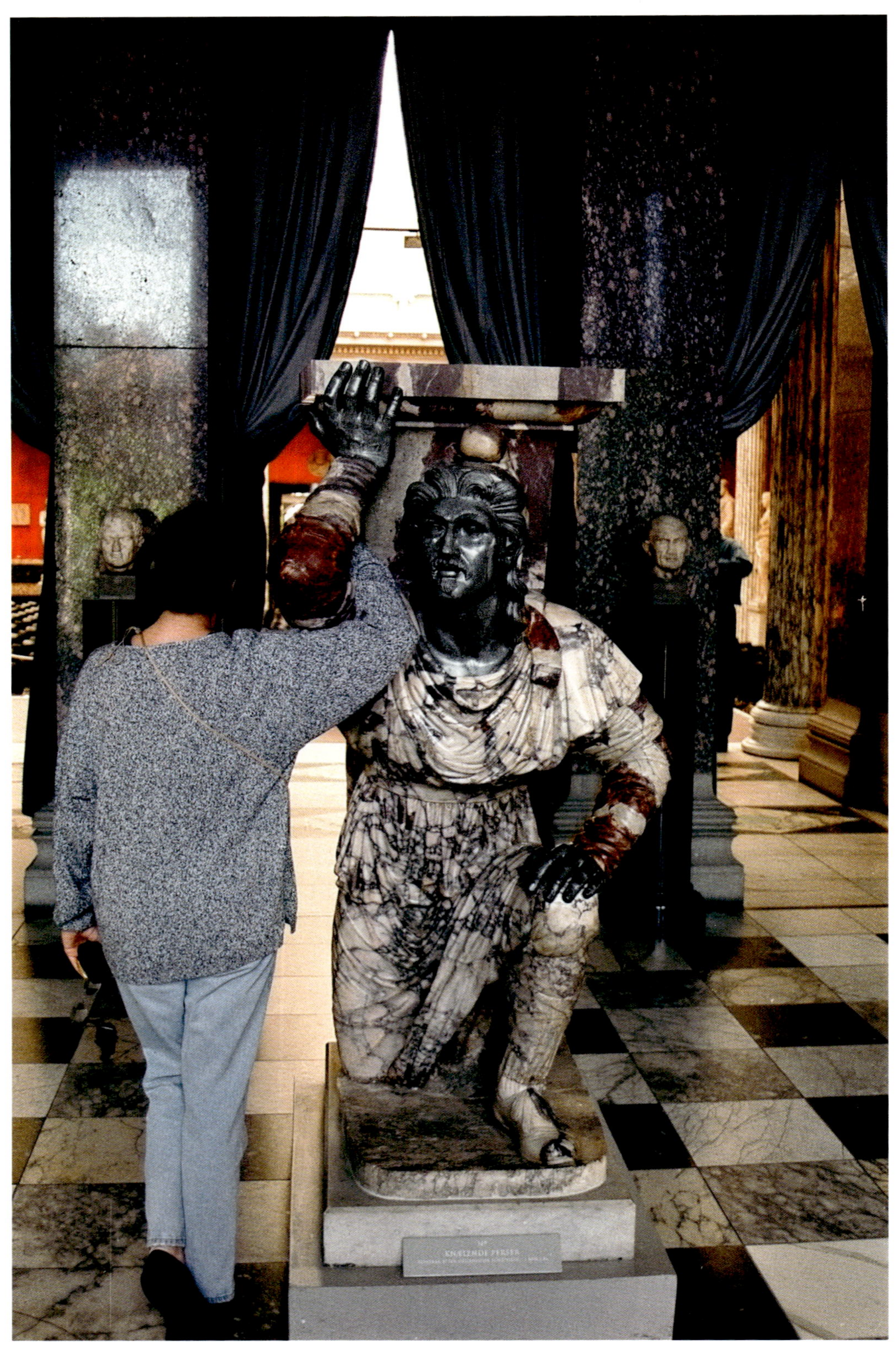

Barbara Z. with Gaul, Glyptotek, Copenhagen, 1997

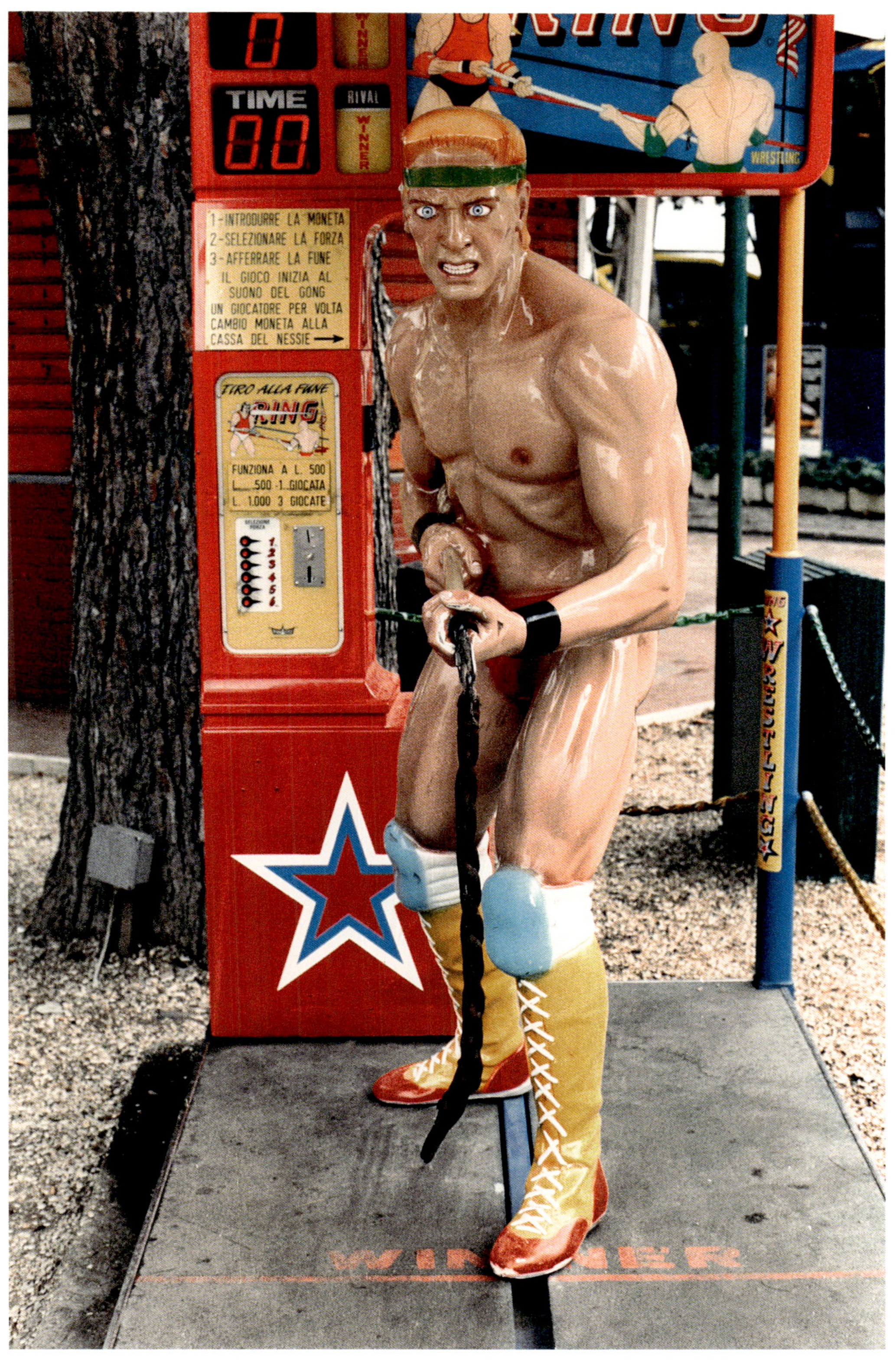

Tug of War, Luna Park, Rome, 1993

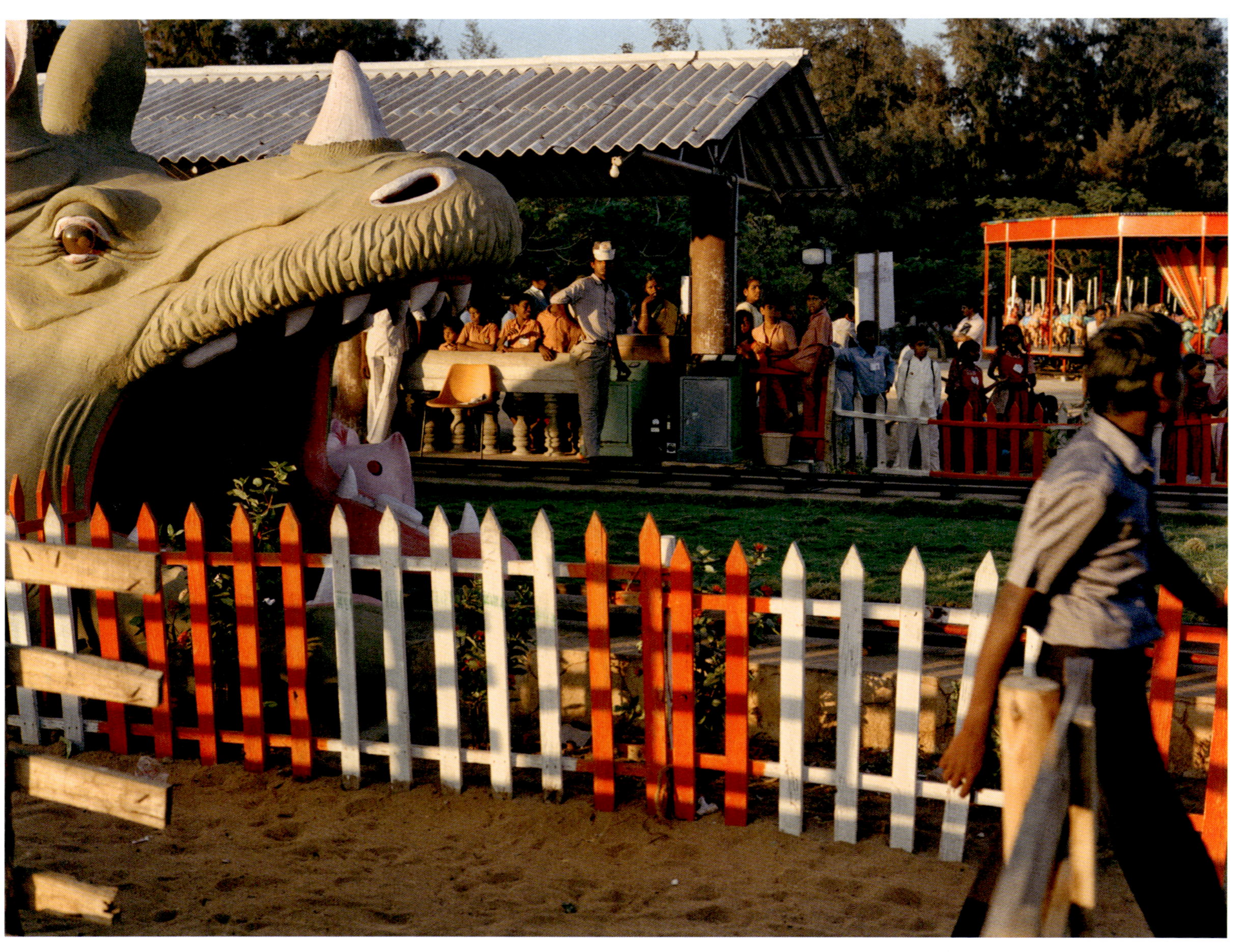

Dinosaur of Mysore, India, 1996

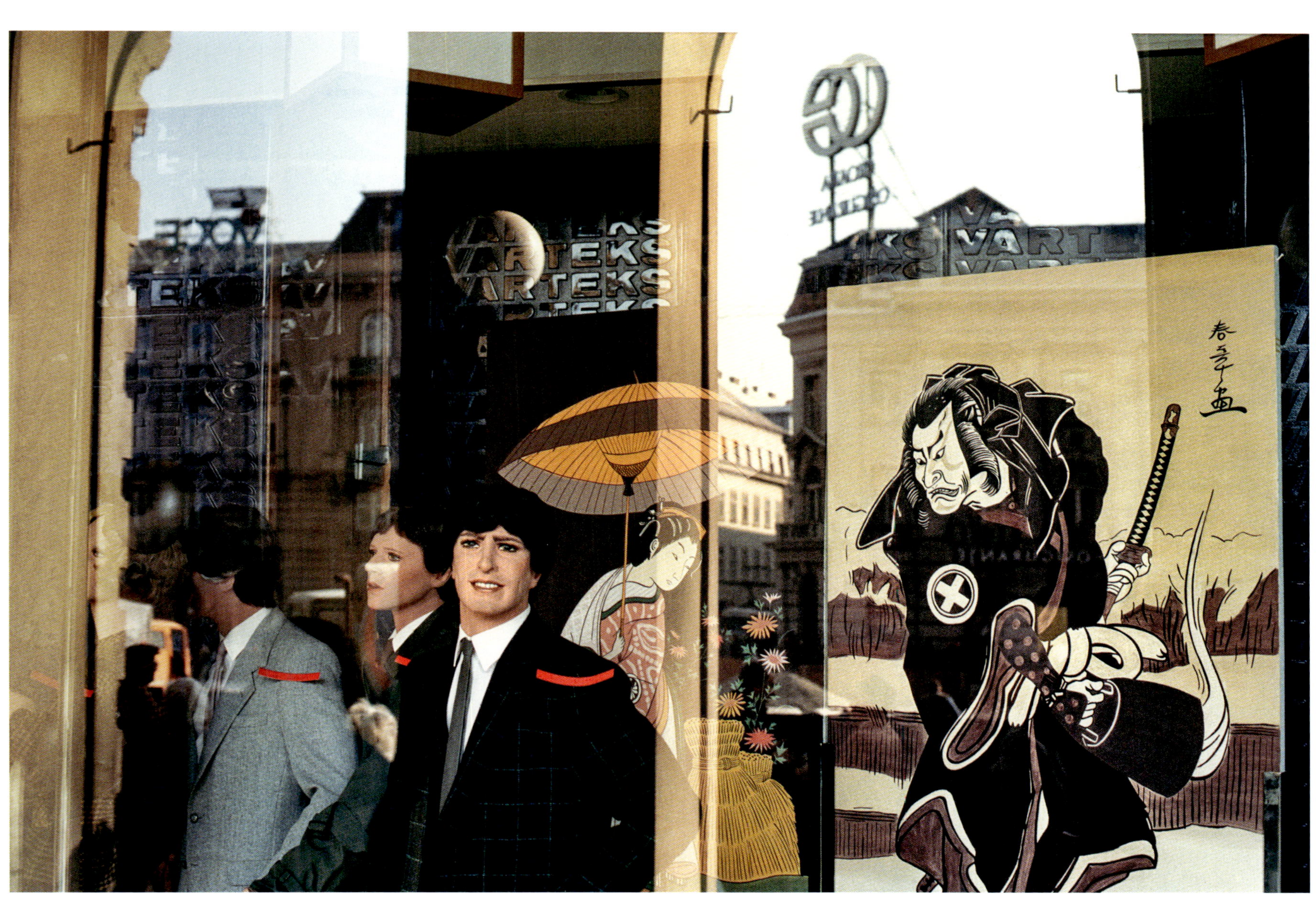

Mannequin and Samurai, Ljubljana, Slovenia, 1985

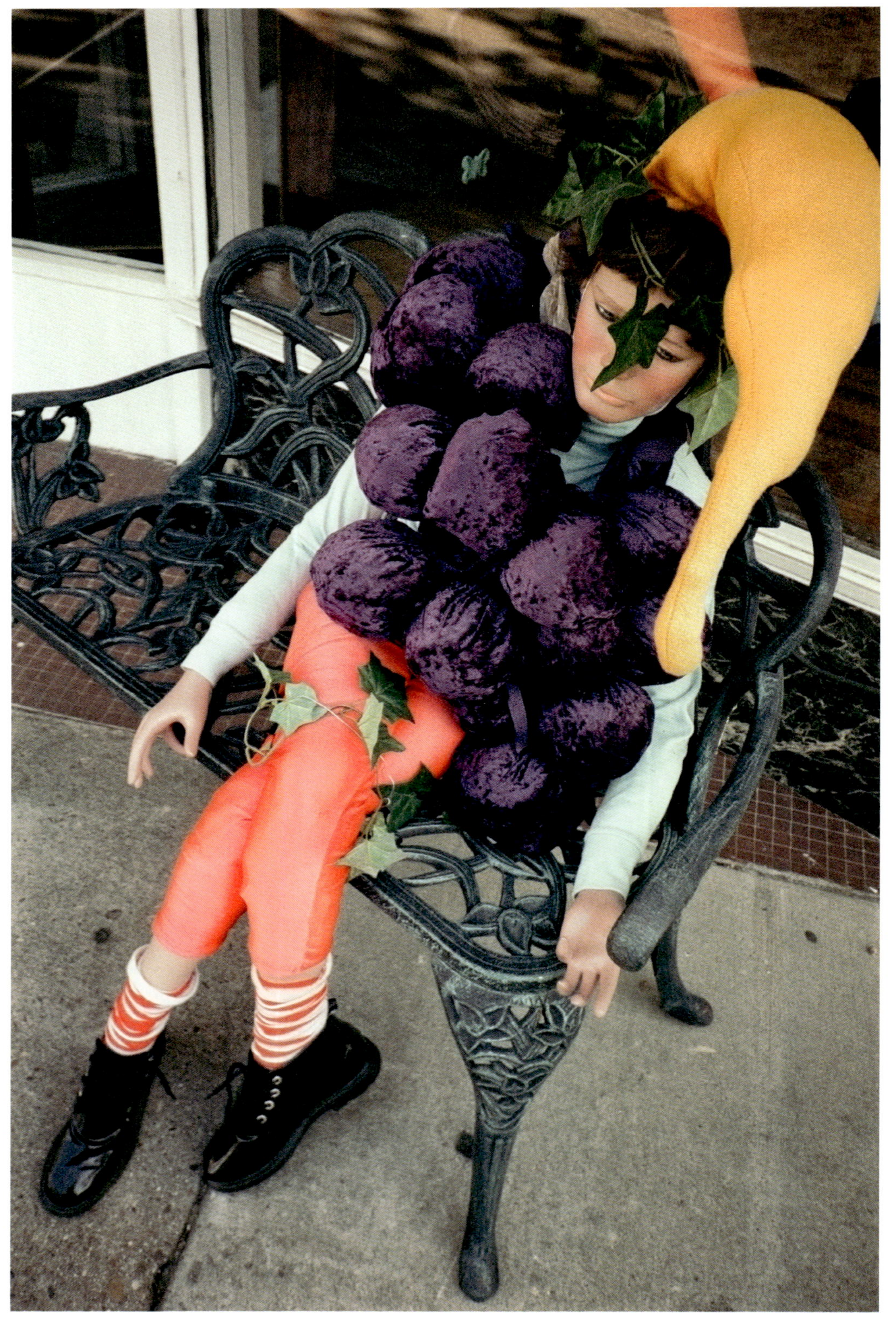

Effigy on Cary Street, Richmond, Virginia, 2000

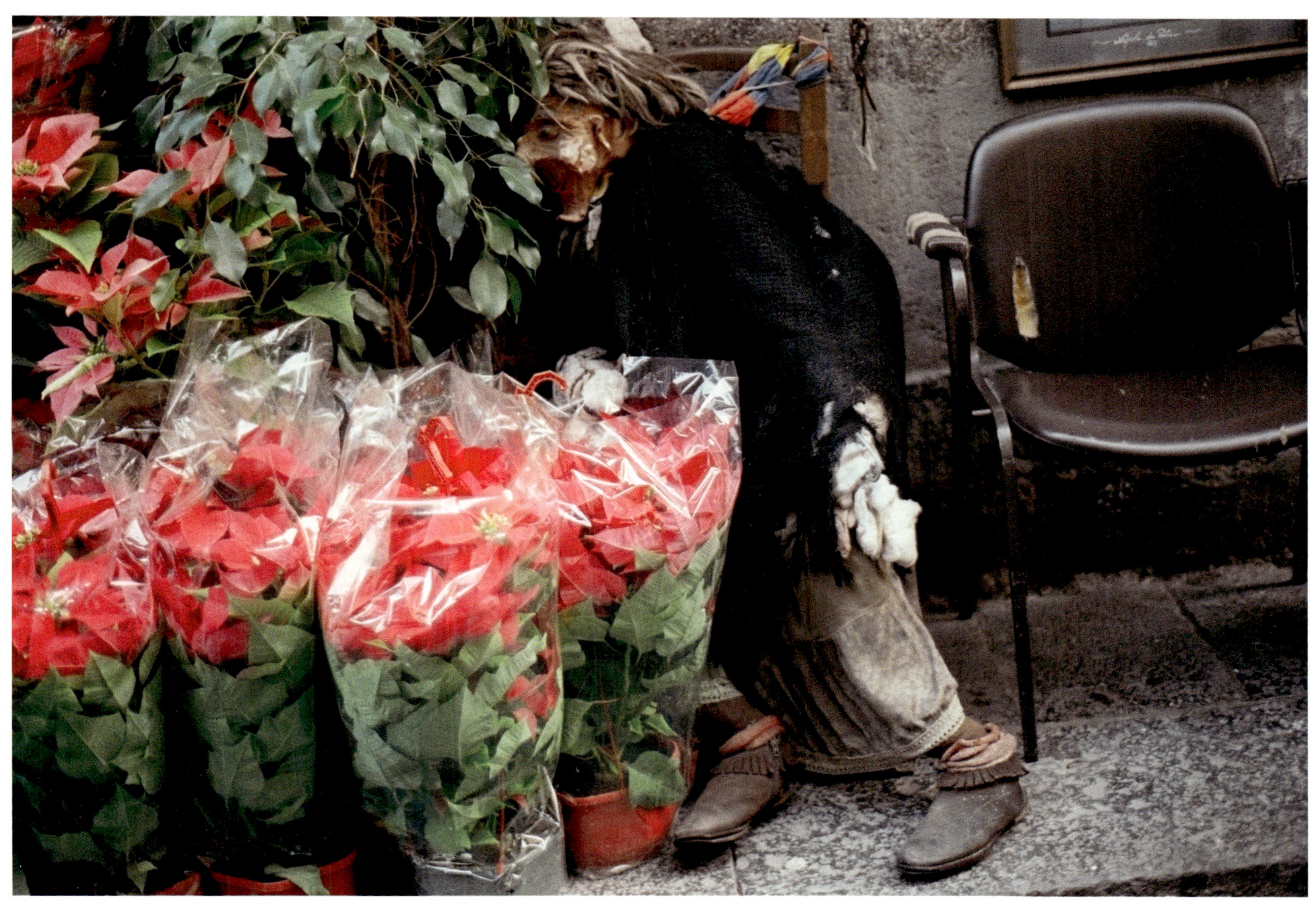

Grotesque Effigy, Naples, 1993

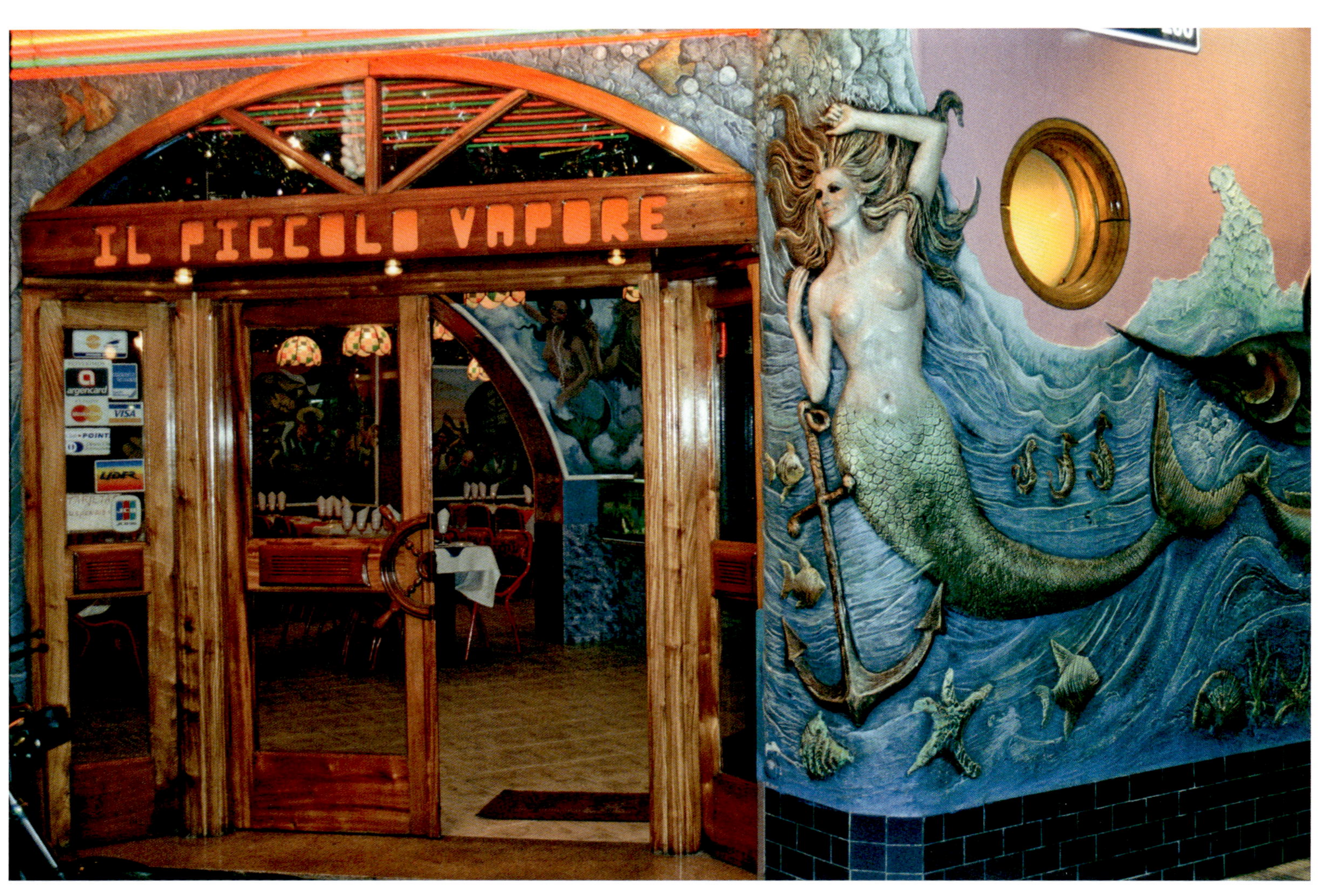

Mermaid Bas-Relief, Buenos Aires, 1980

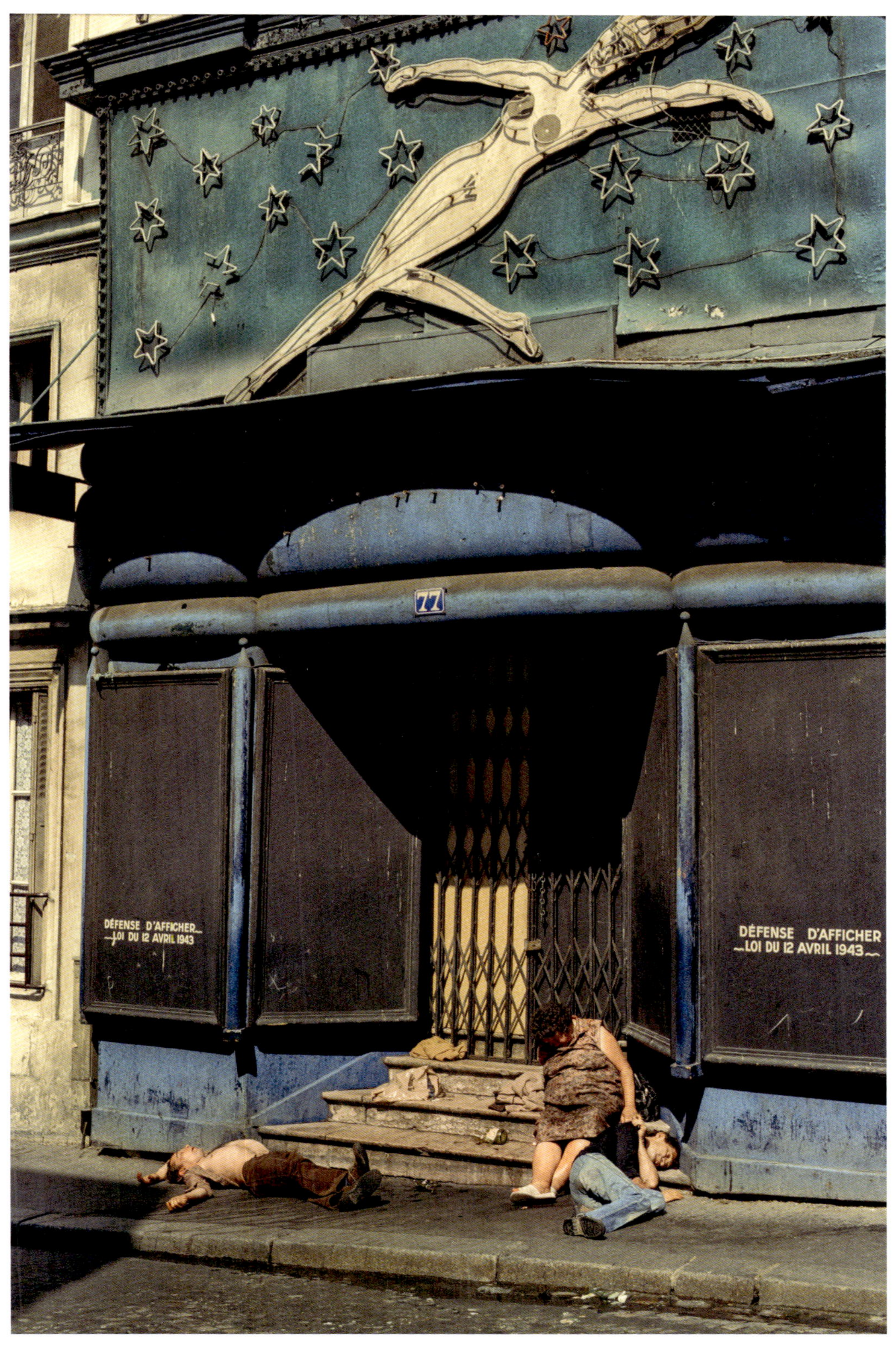

Near Place St. Georges, Paris, 1983

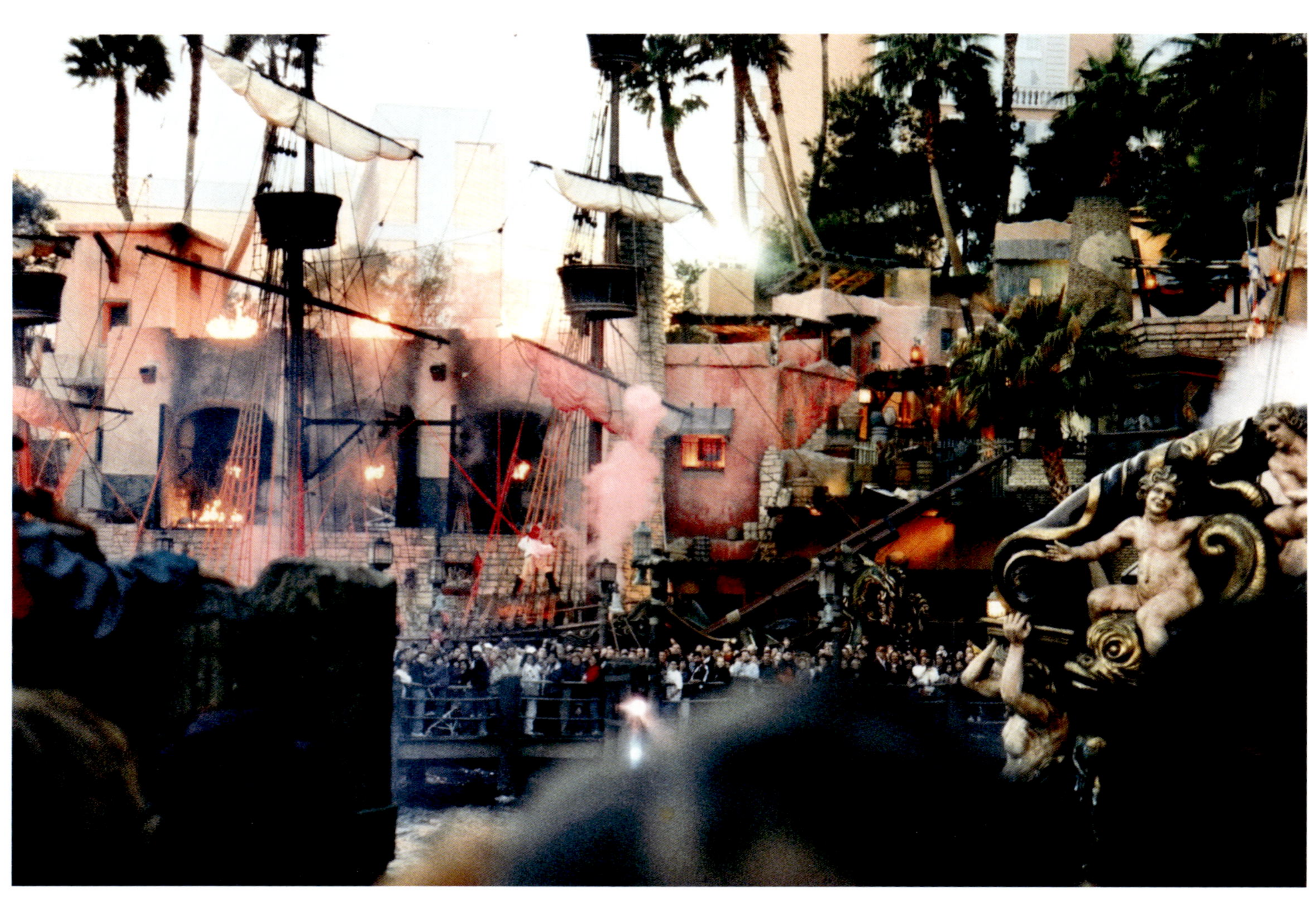

Pirate Ship Mockup, Las Vegas, 1999

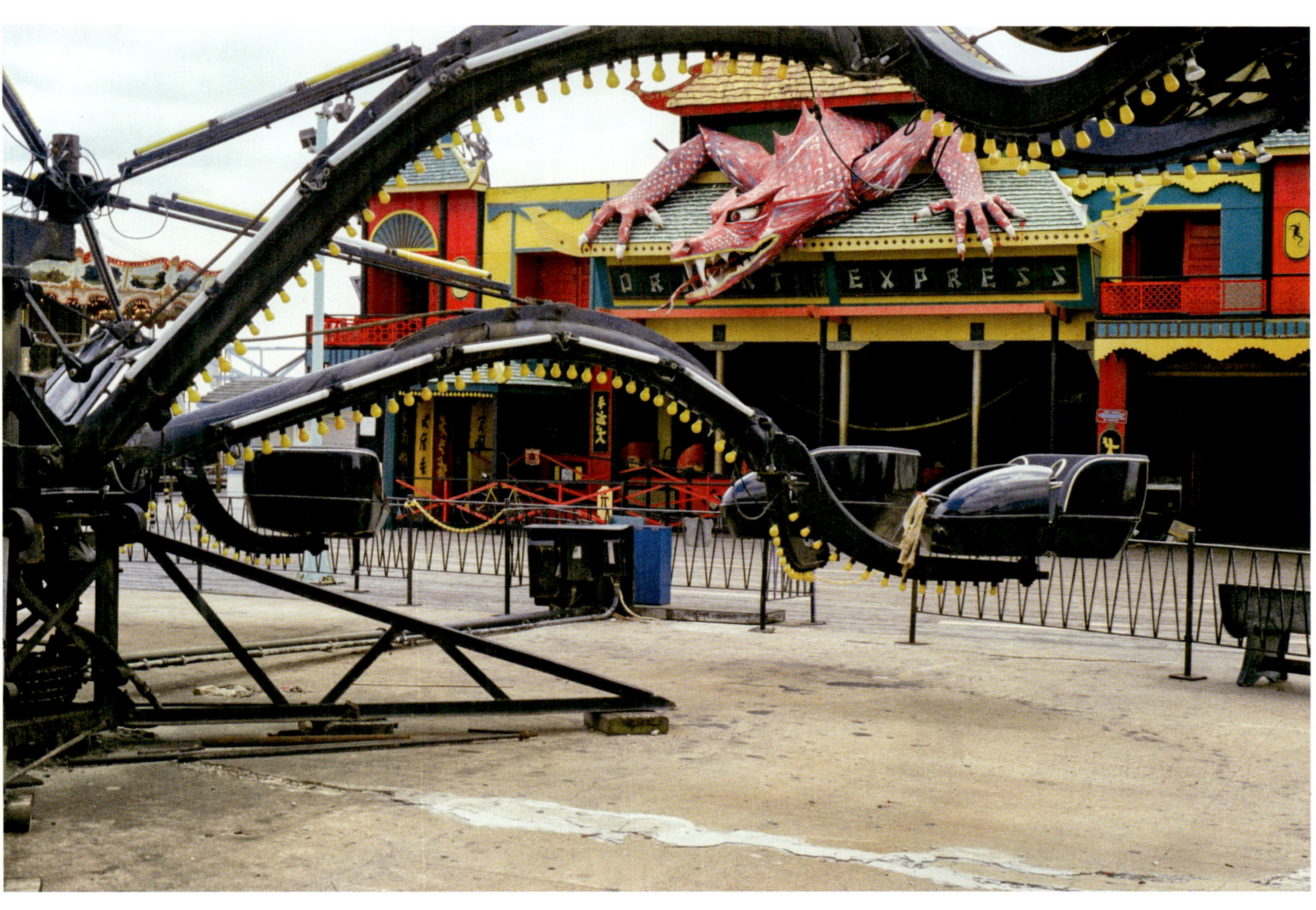

Atlantic City Dragon, 1987

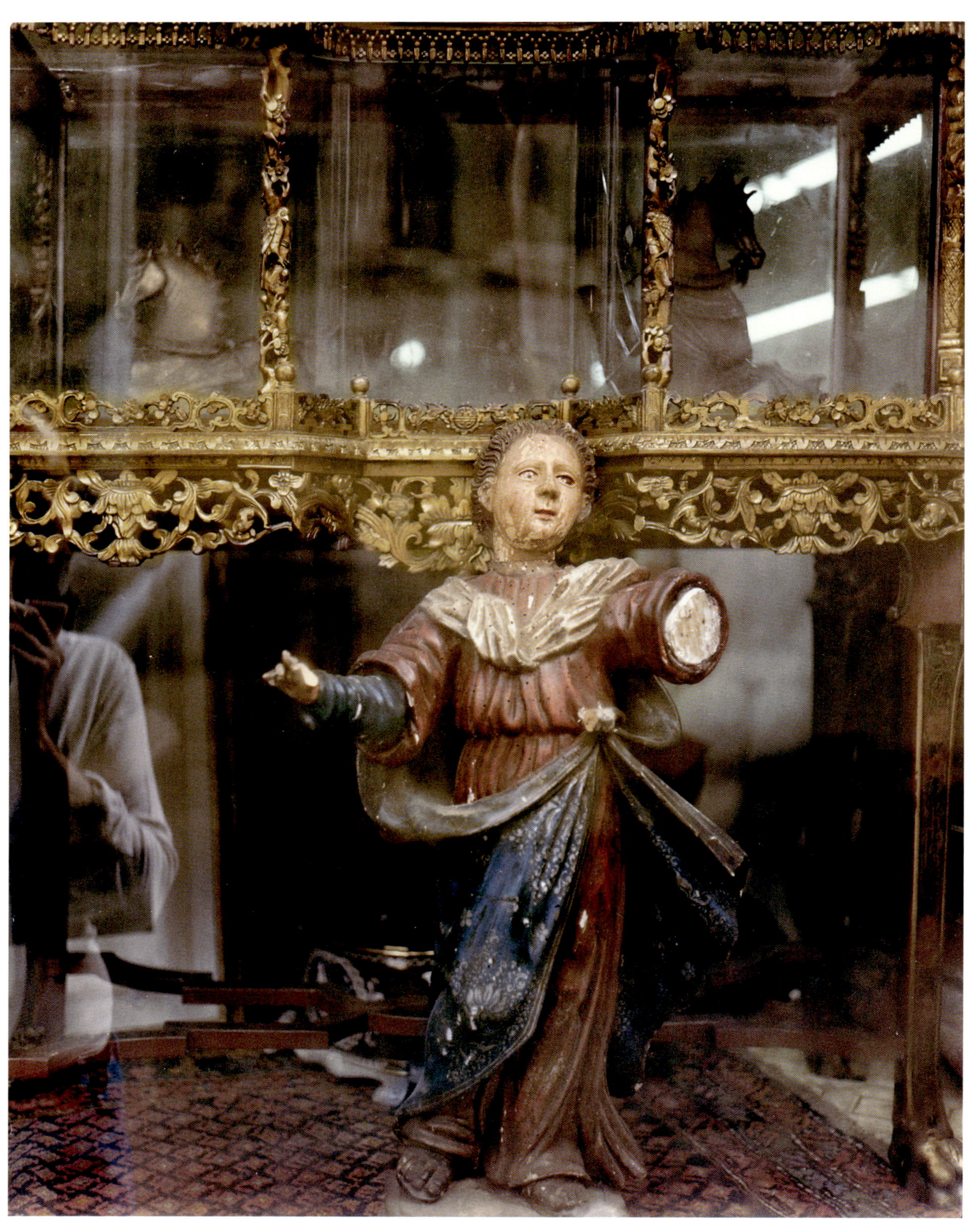

Disconnected Angel, New York, 1978

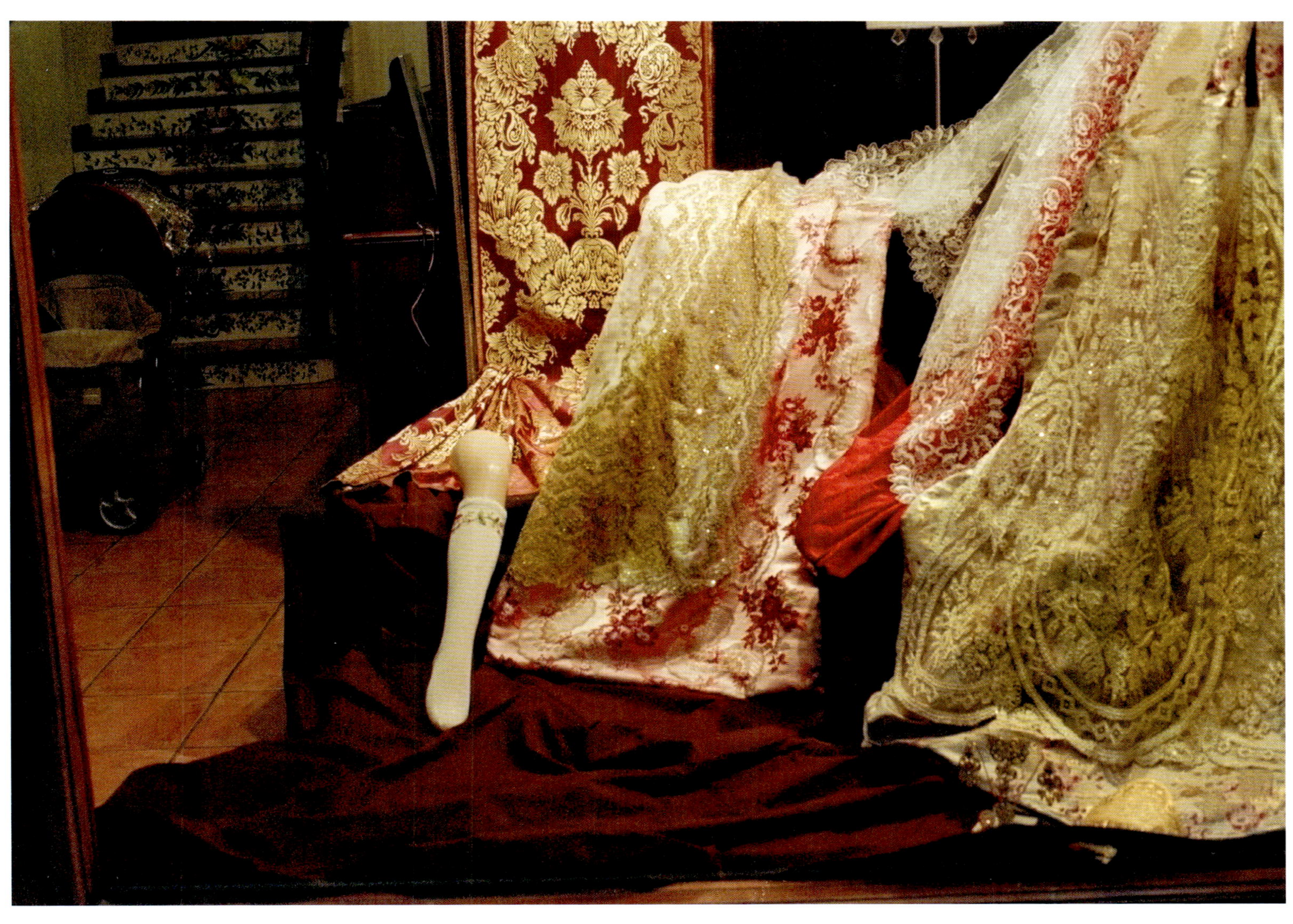

Leg, Valencia, Spain, 2008

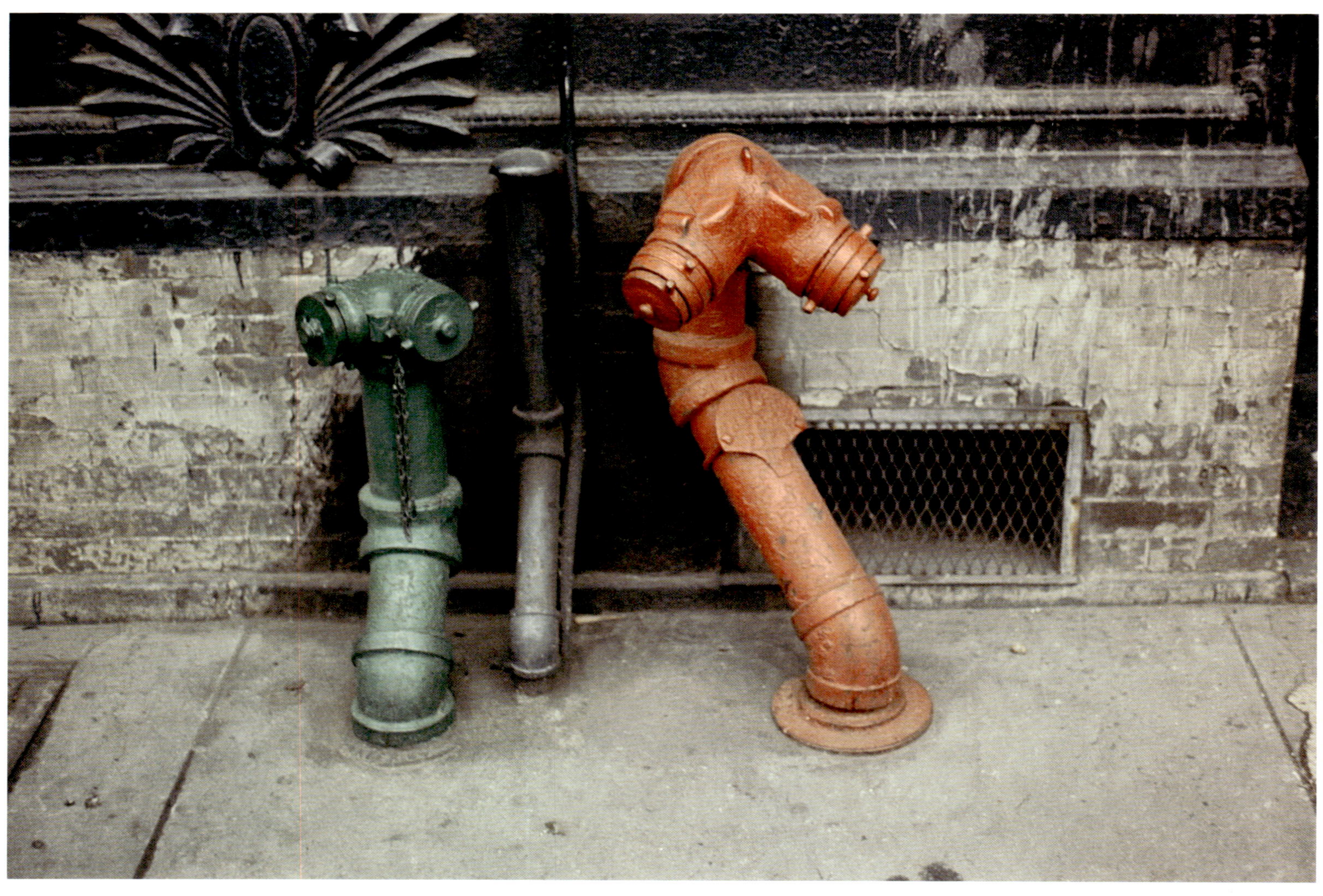

Romeo and Juliet, New York, 1977

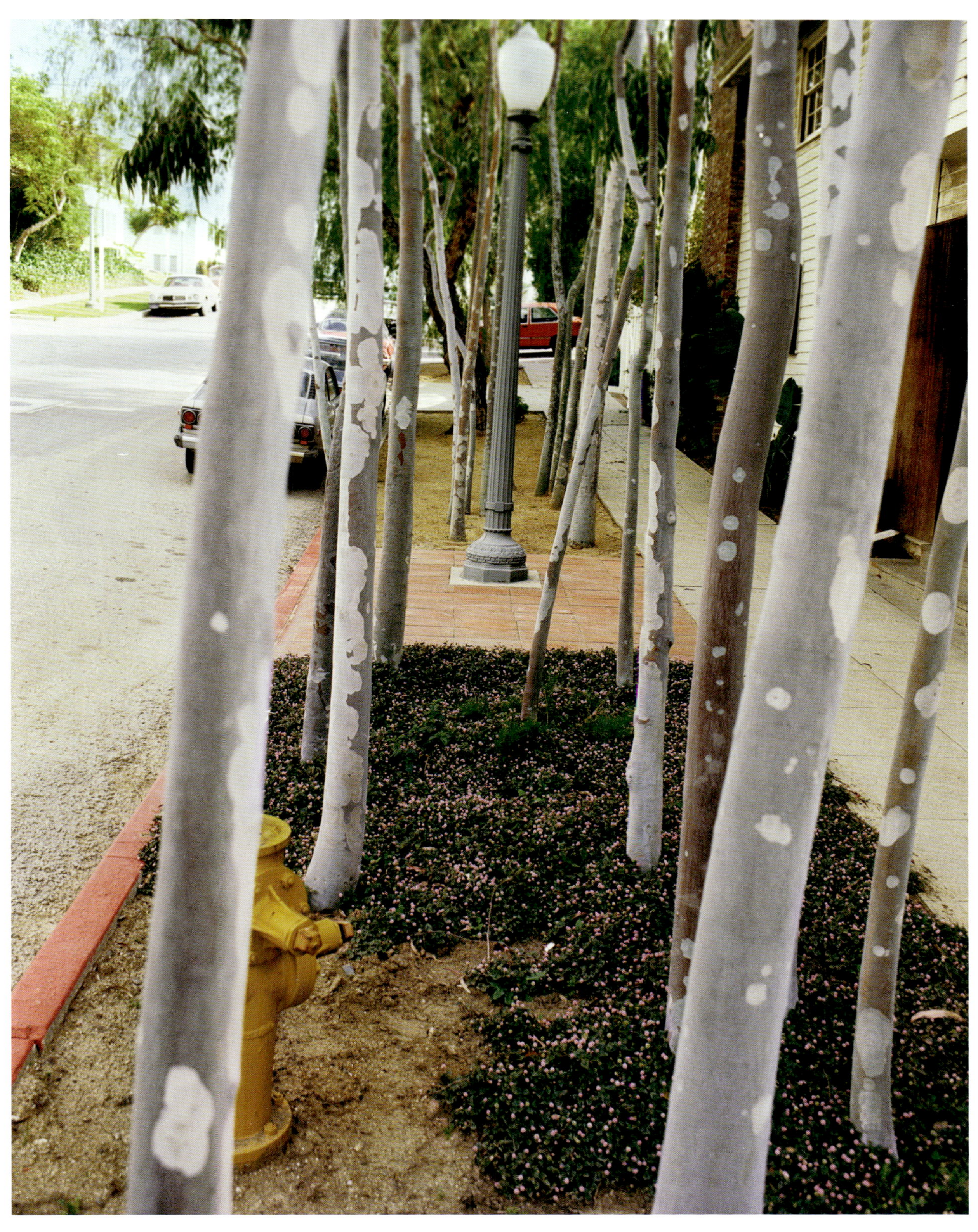

Yellow Fire Hydrant, Los Angeles, 1979

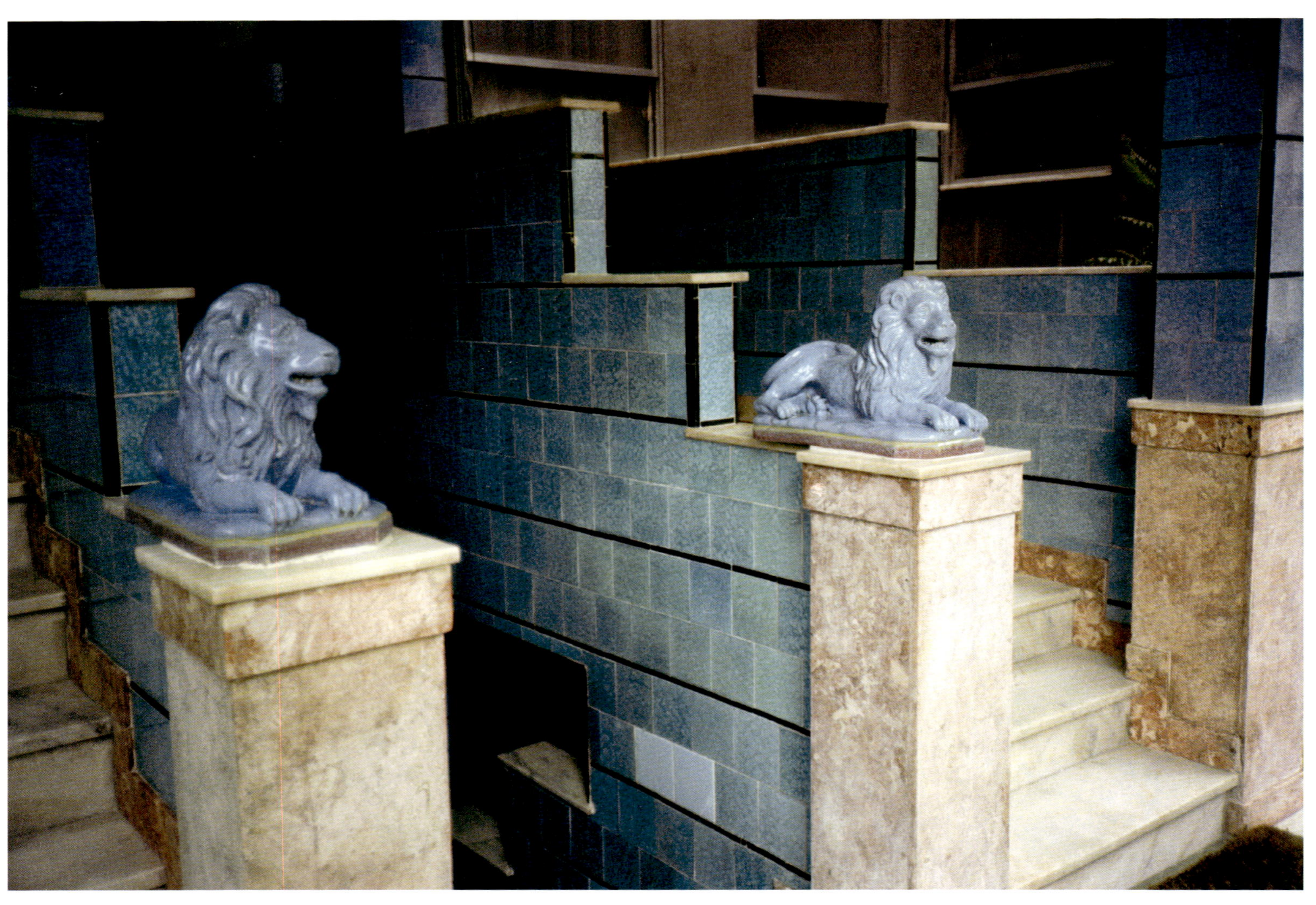

Apartment Entrance, Rio de Janeiro, 1980

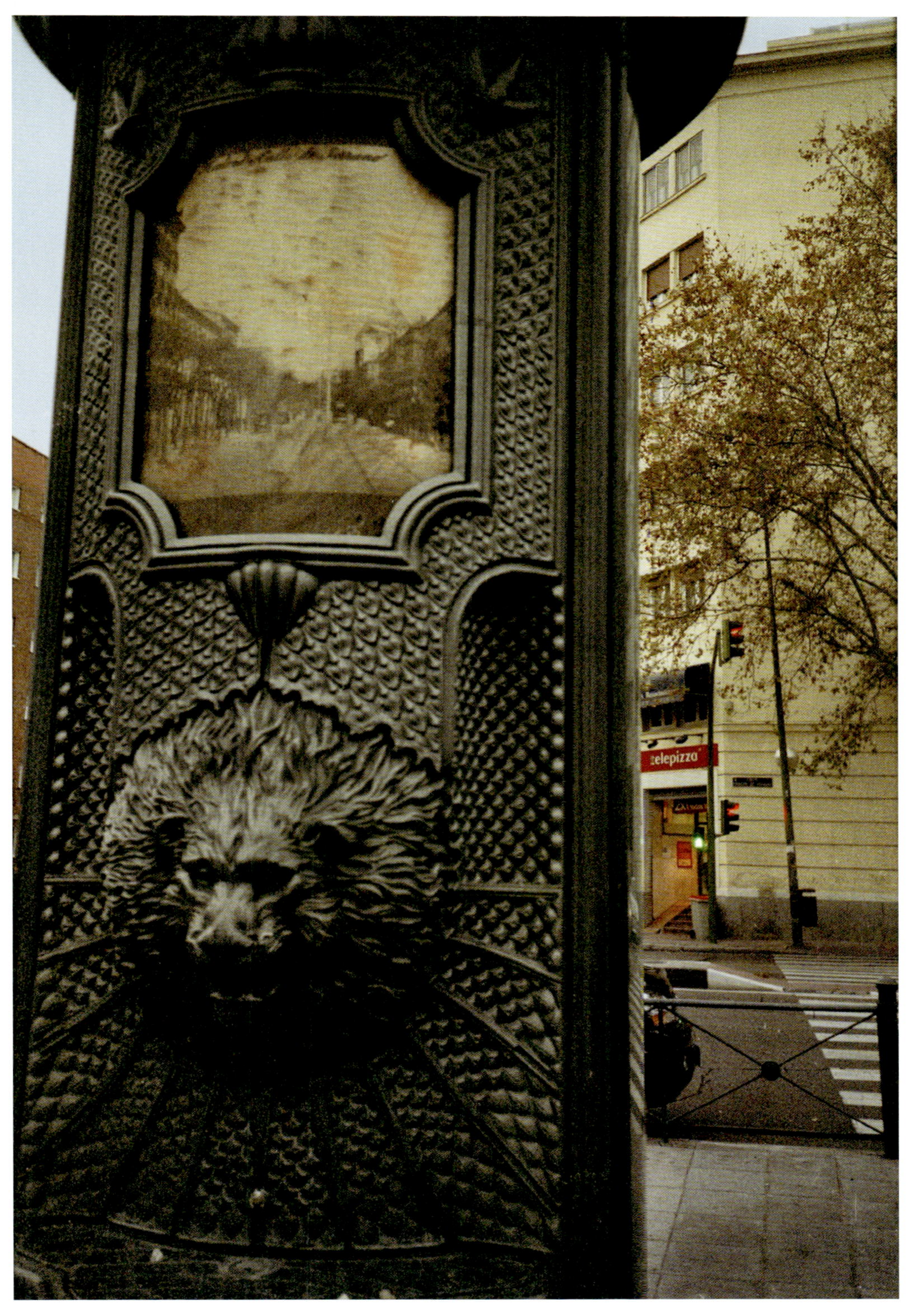

Lion Bas-Relief, Madrid, 2007

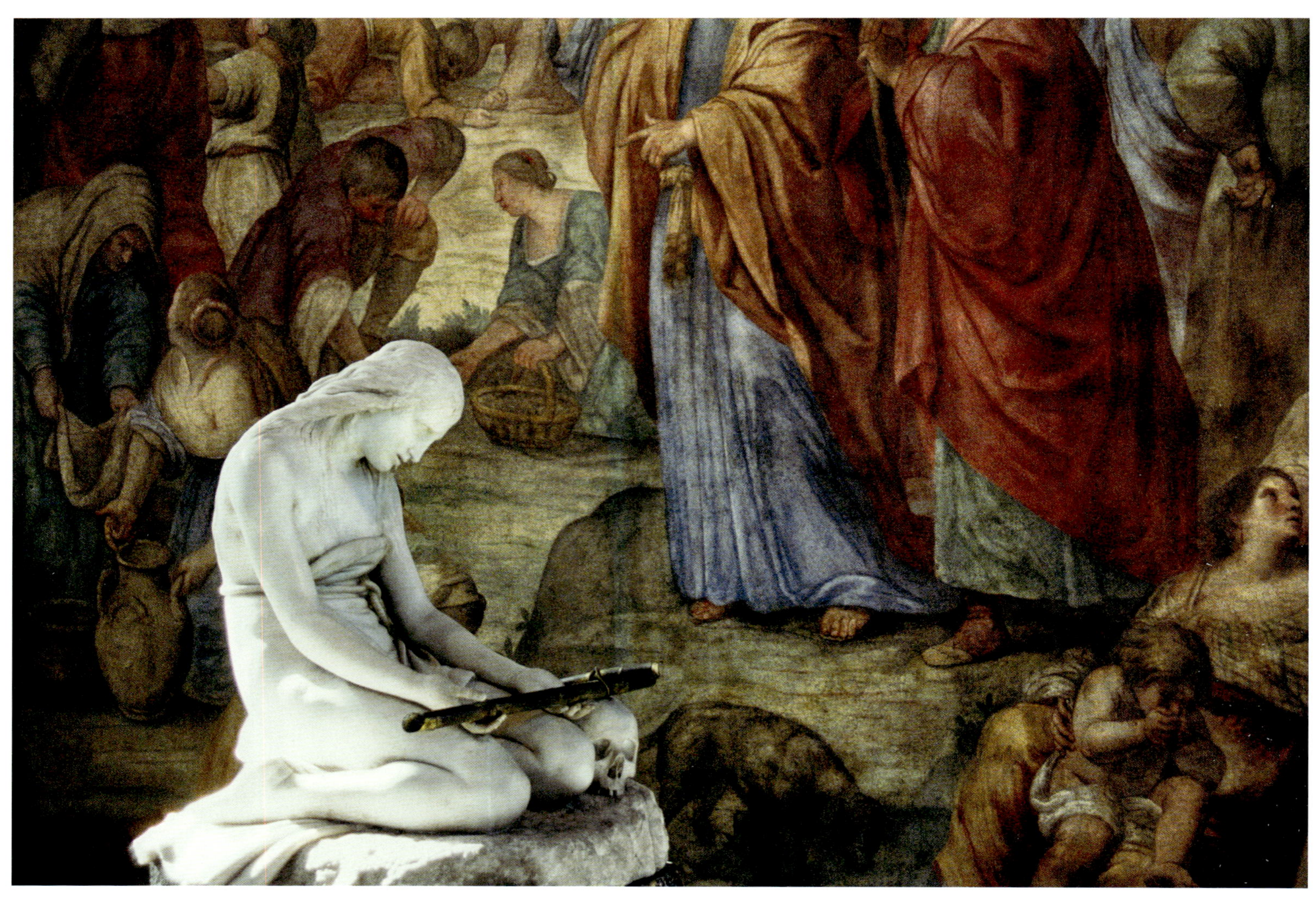

Repentant Mary Magdalene, Italy, 2000

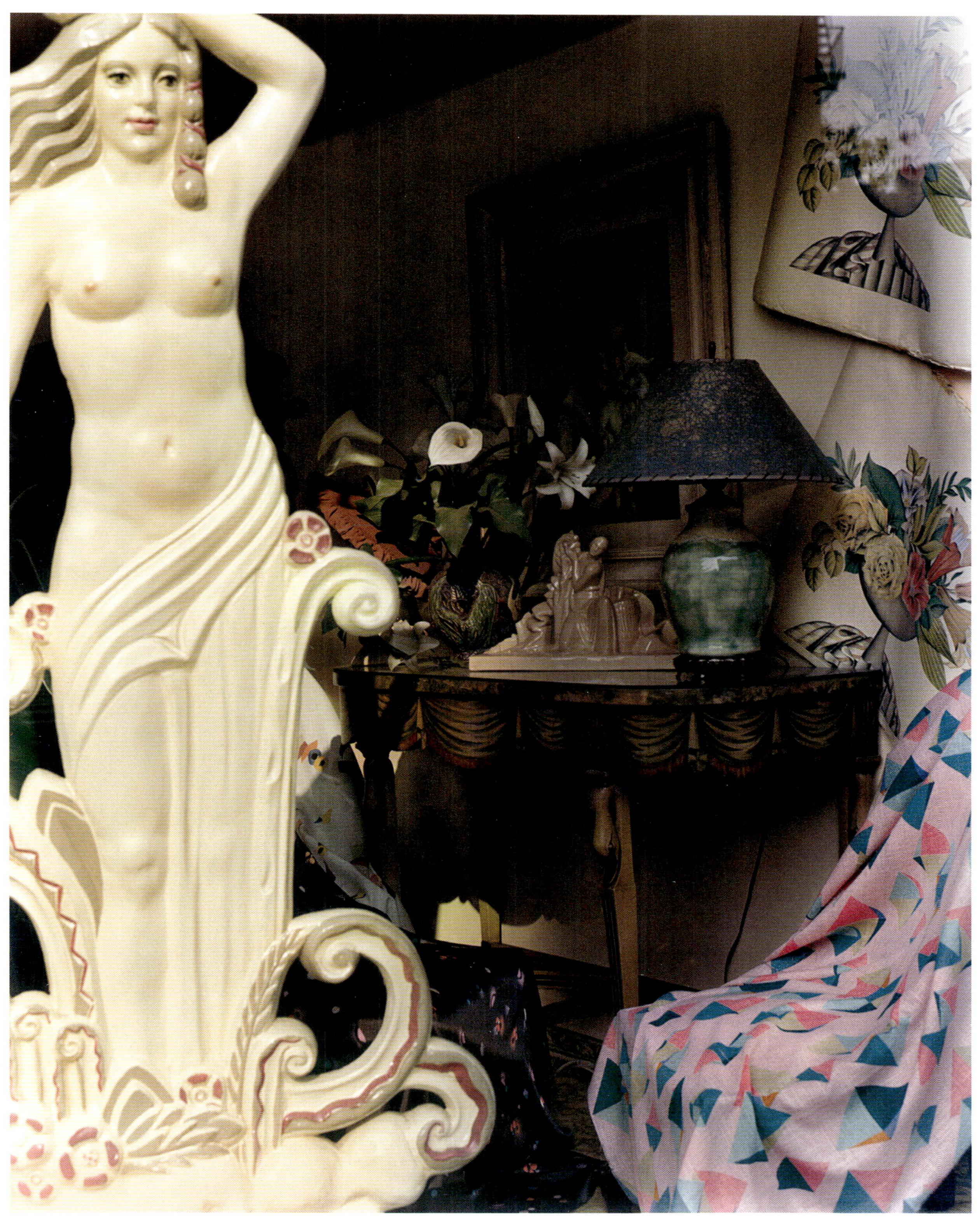

Art Deco Interior, West Village, New York, 1980

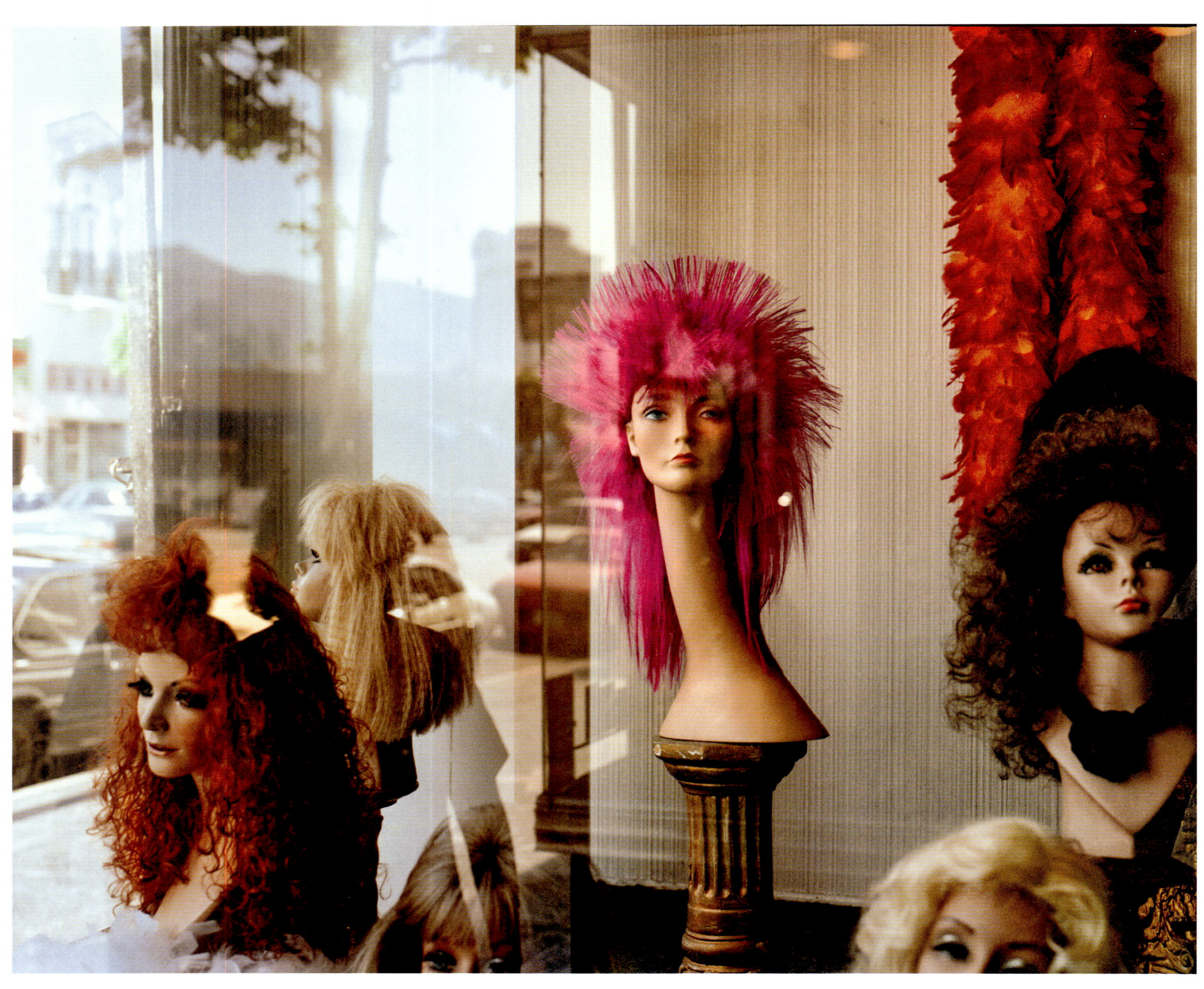

Mannequin with a Long Neck, Miami, 1989

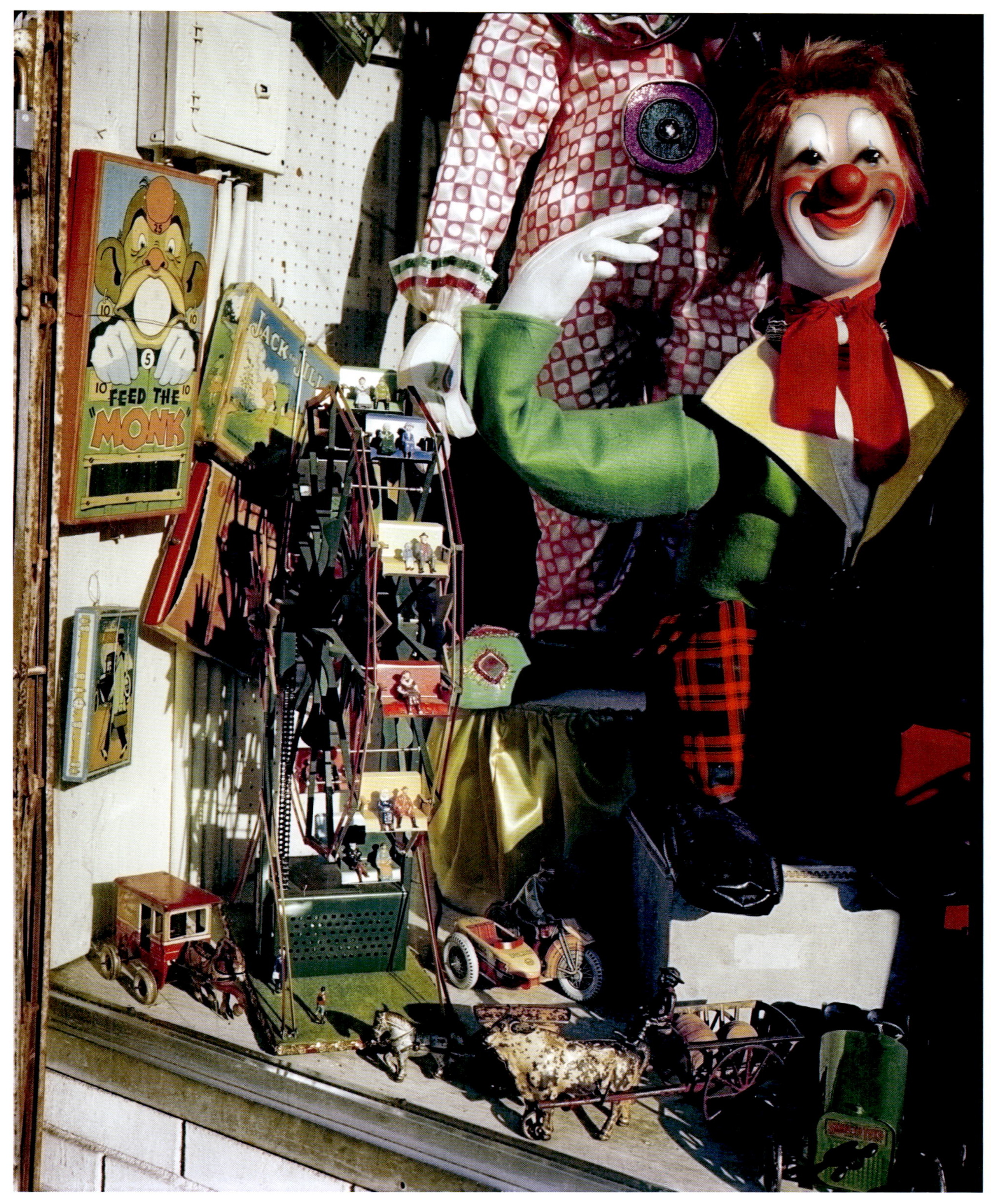

Clown With Ferris Wheel, New York, 1978

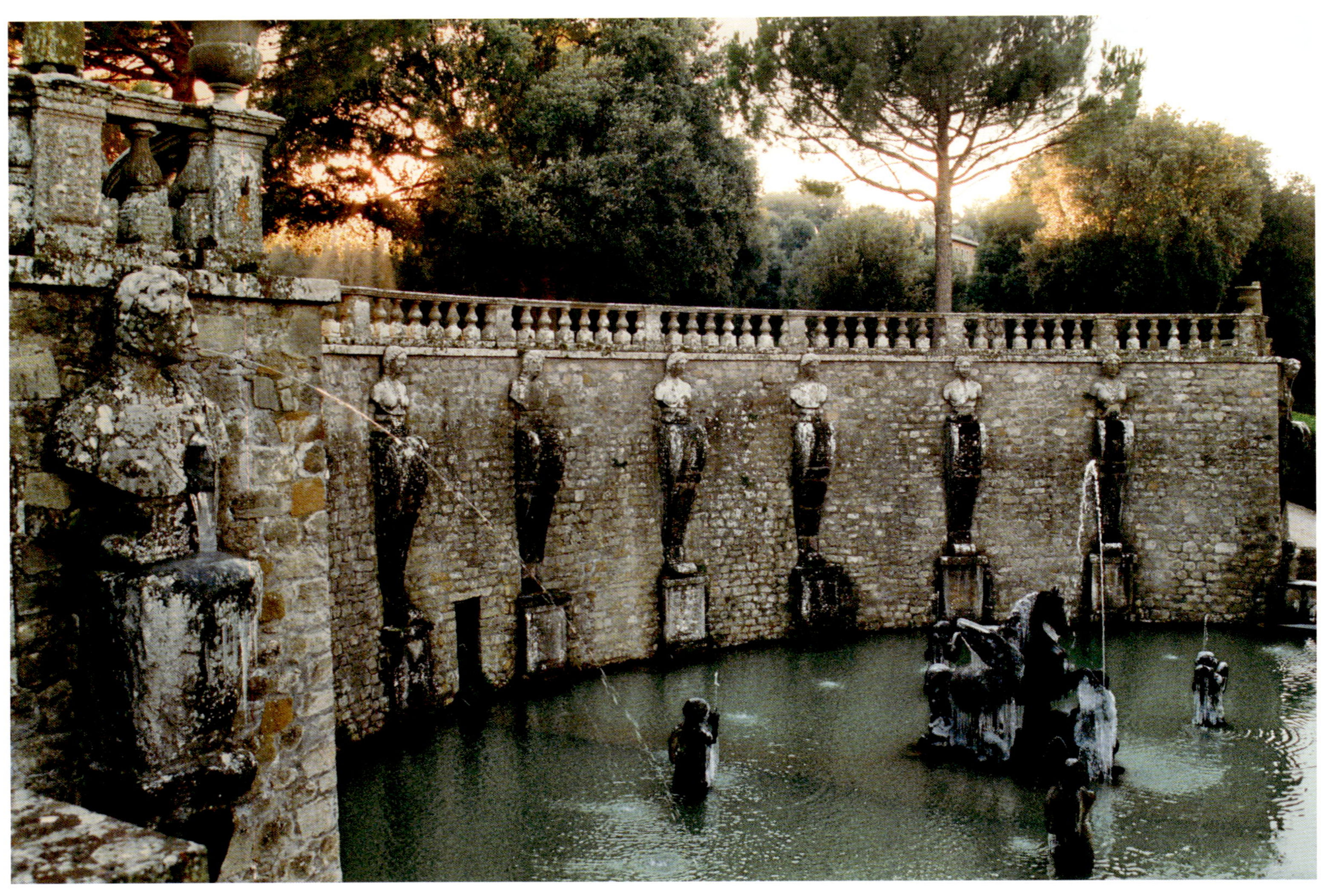

Statues Spitting Water, Villa Lante, Italy, 2000

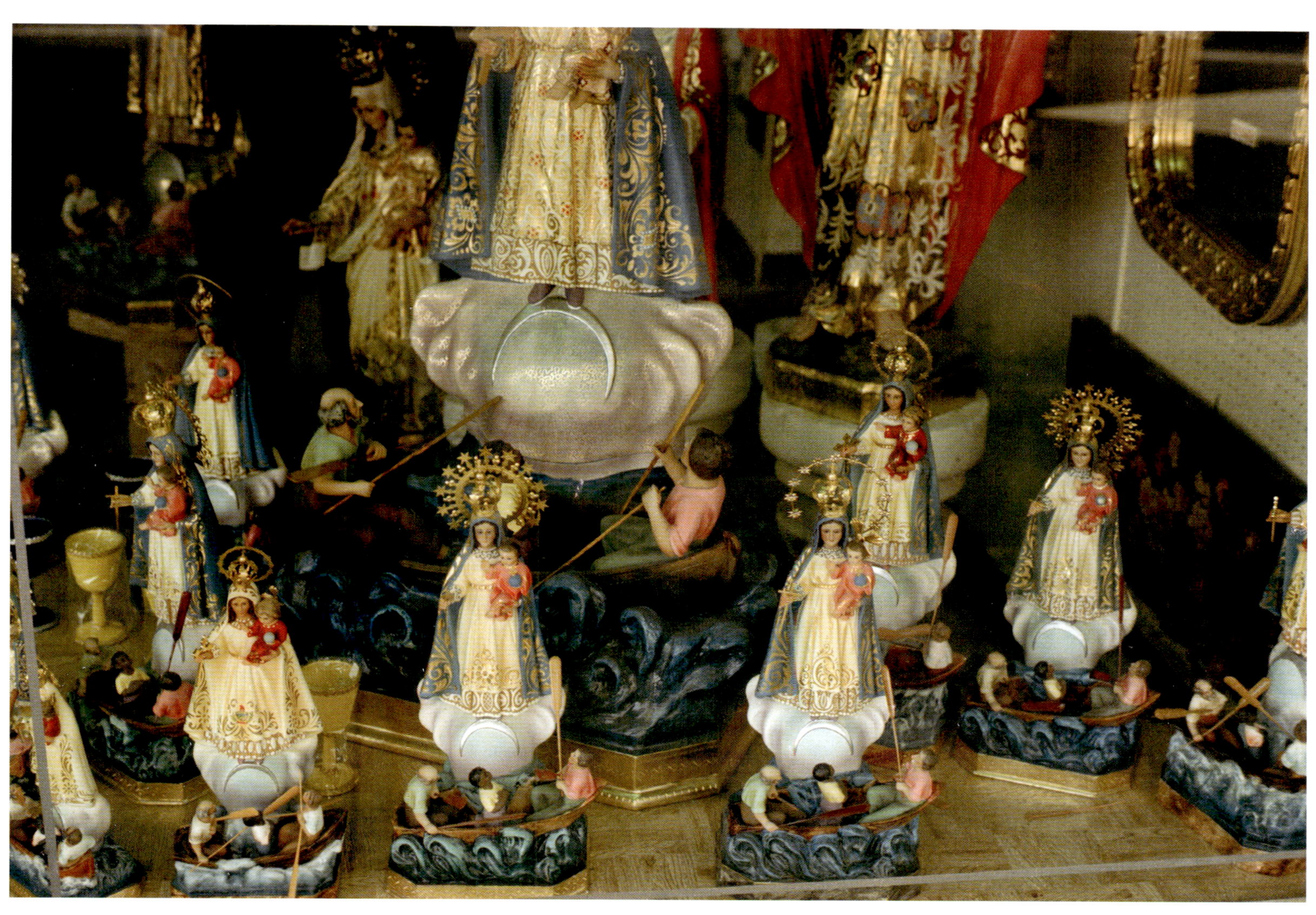

Religious Goods, Miami, 1977

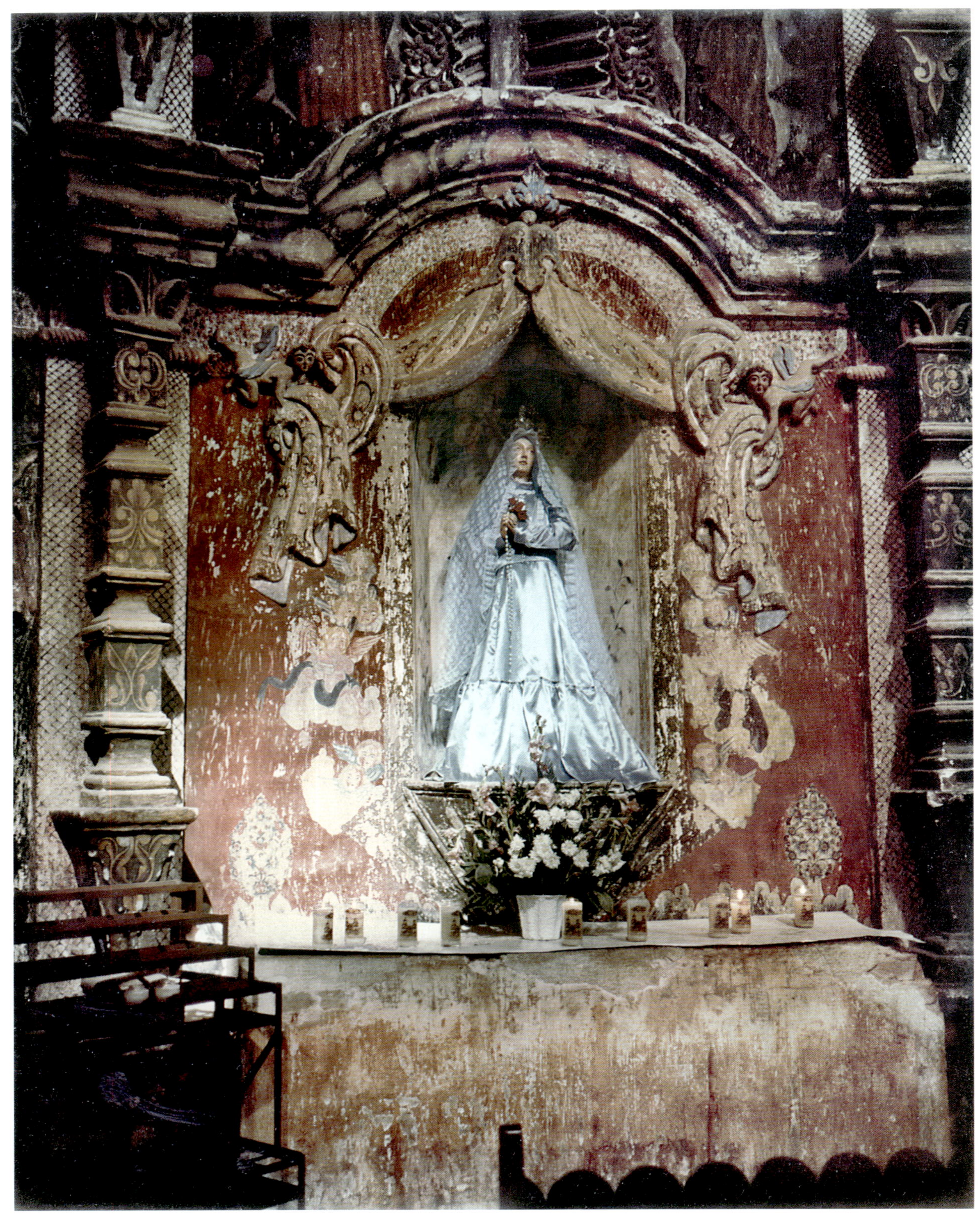

Dolores Mission, Tucson, 1979

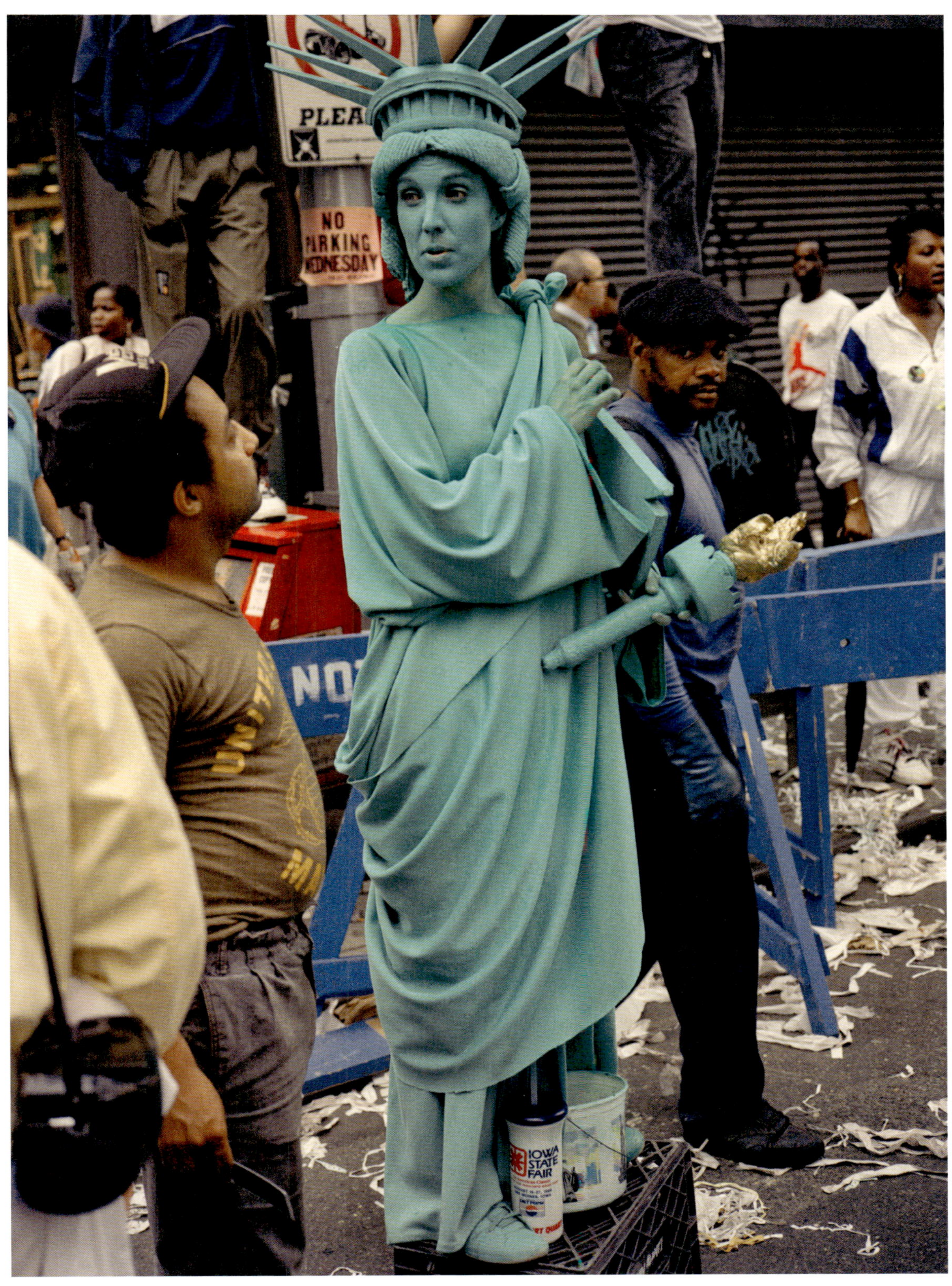

Liberty at Mandela Parade, New York, 1990

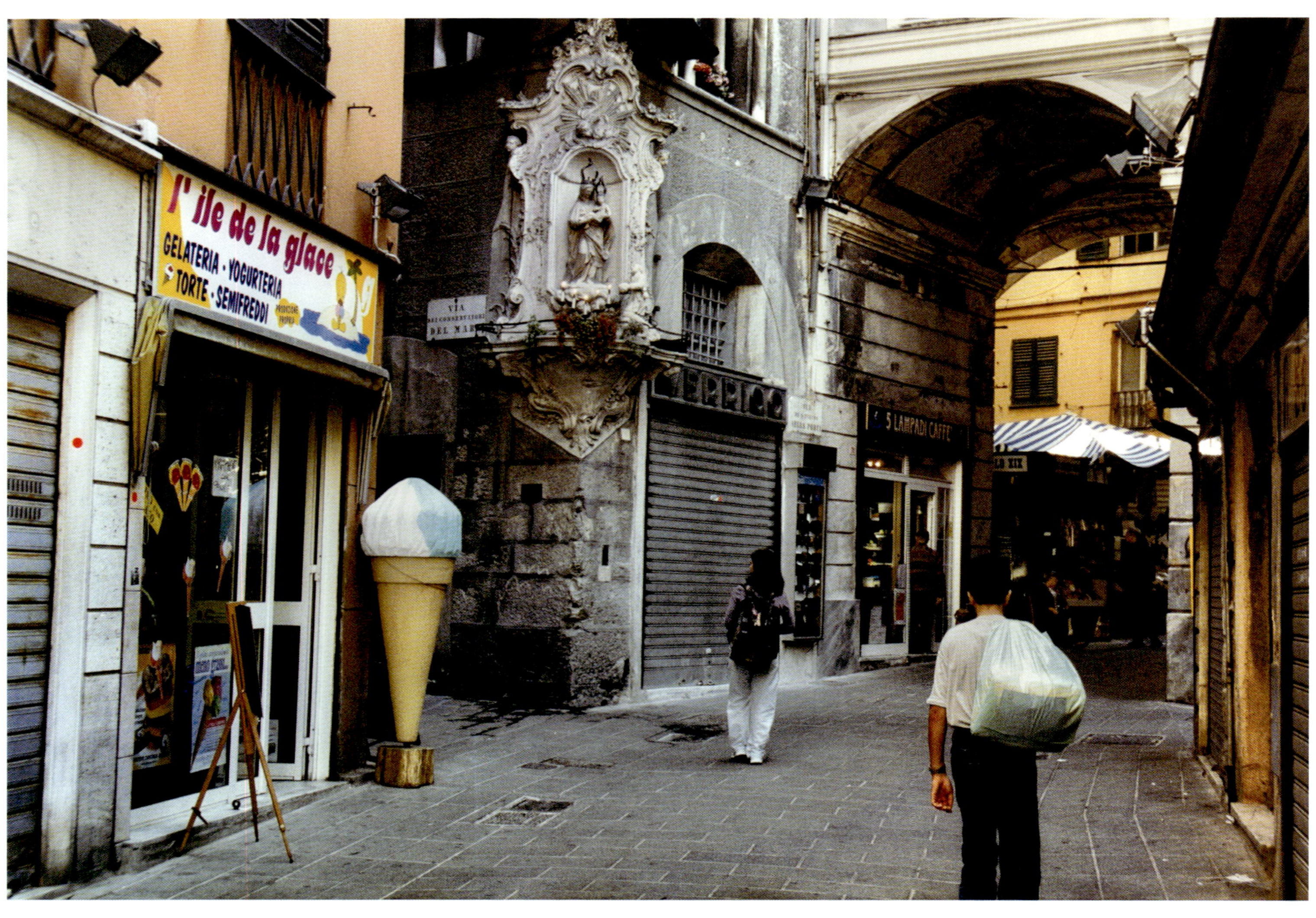

Via della Porta, Genoa, 2001

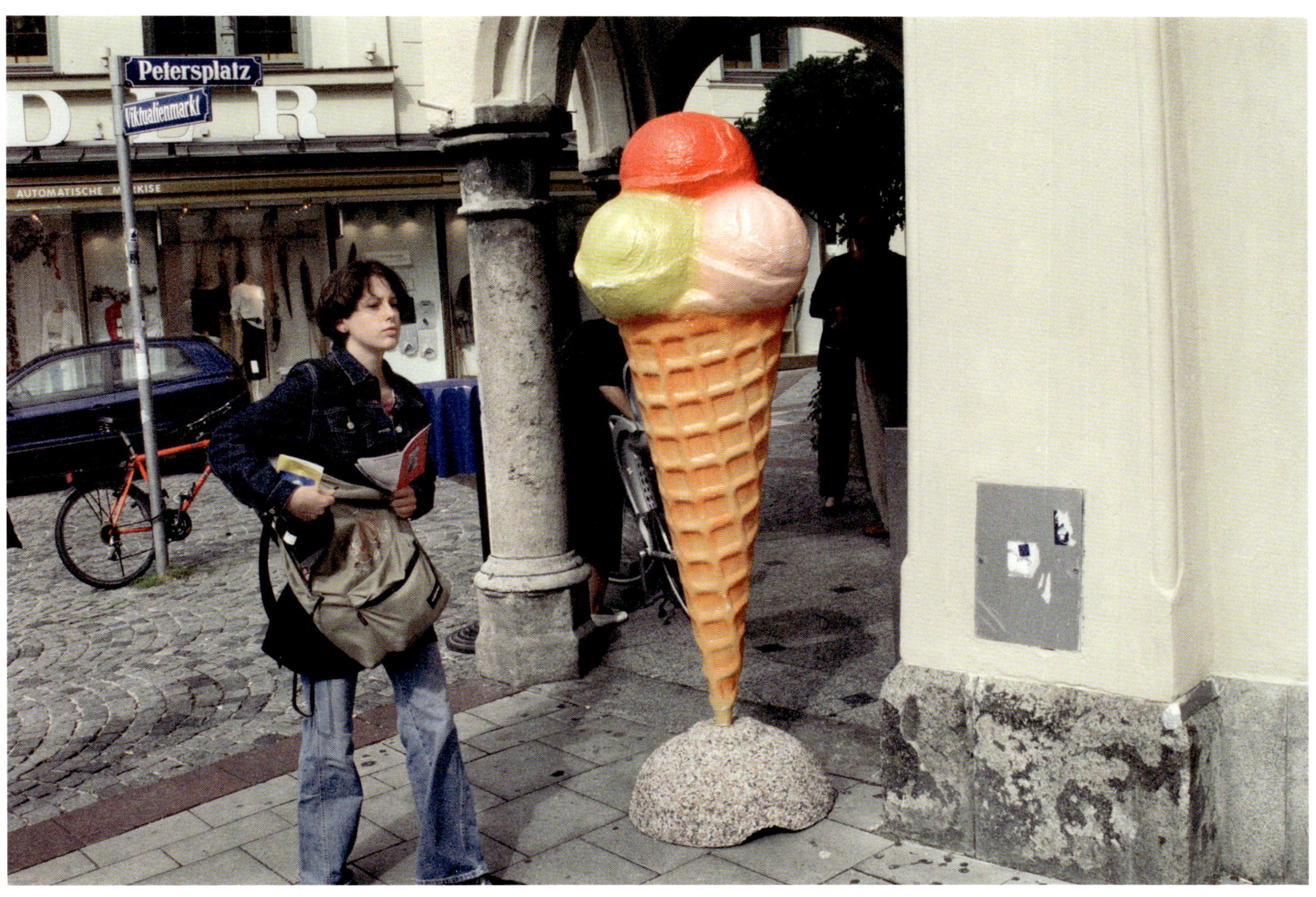

Ice Cream Cone, Munich, 2003

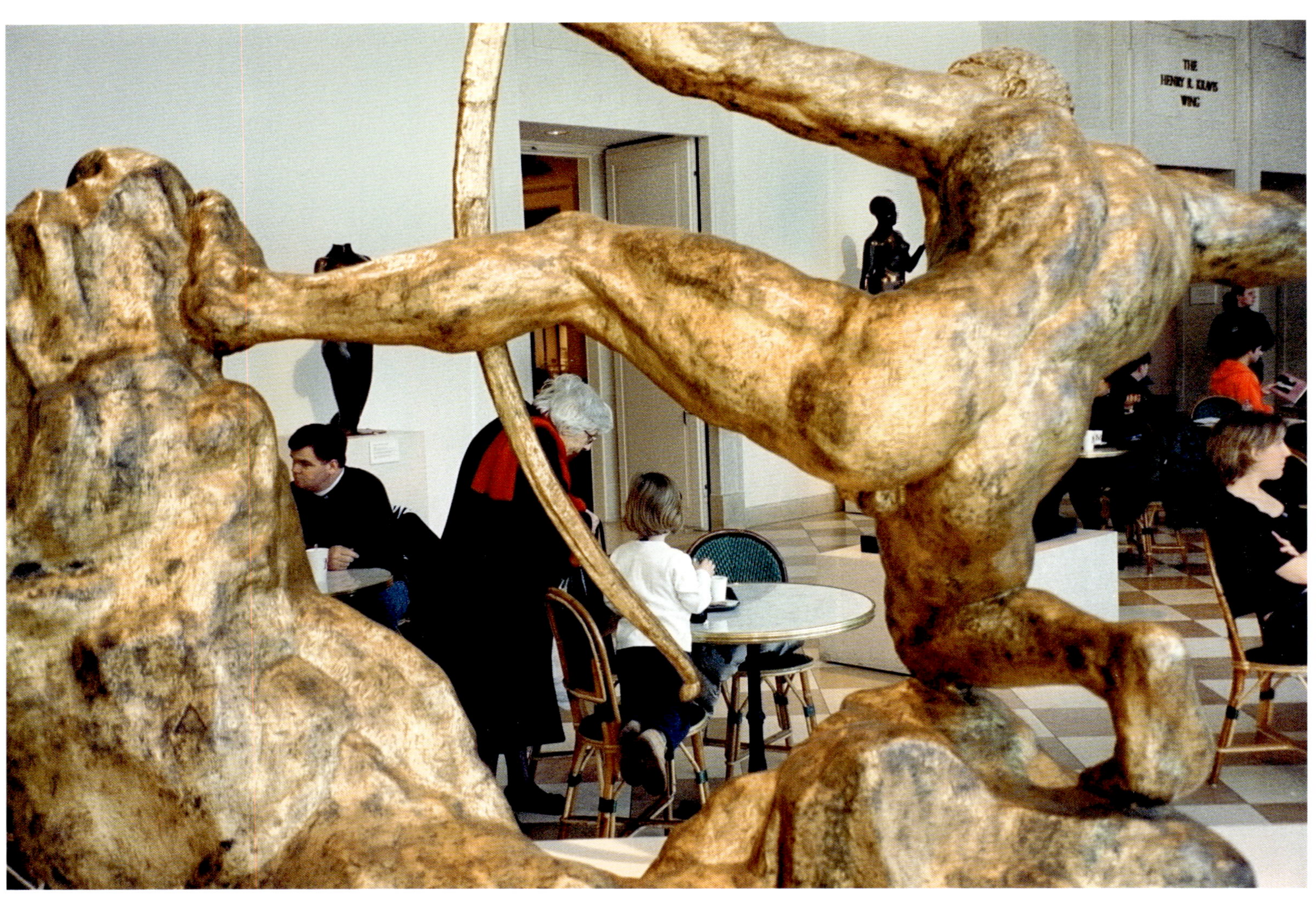

Cafe at the Metropolitan Museum, Antoine-Emile Bourdelle, New York, 2002

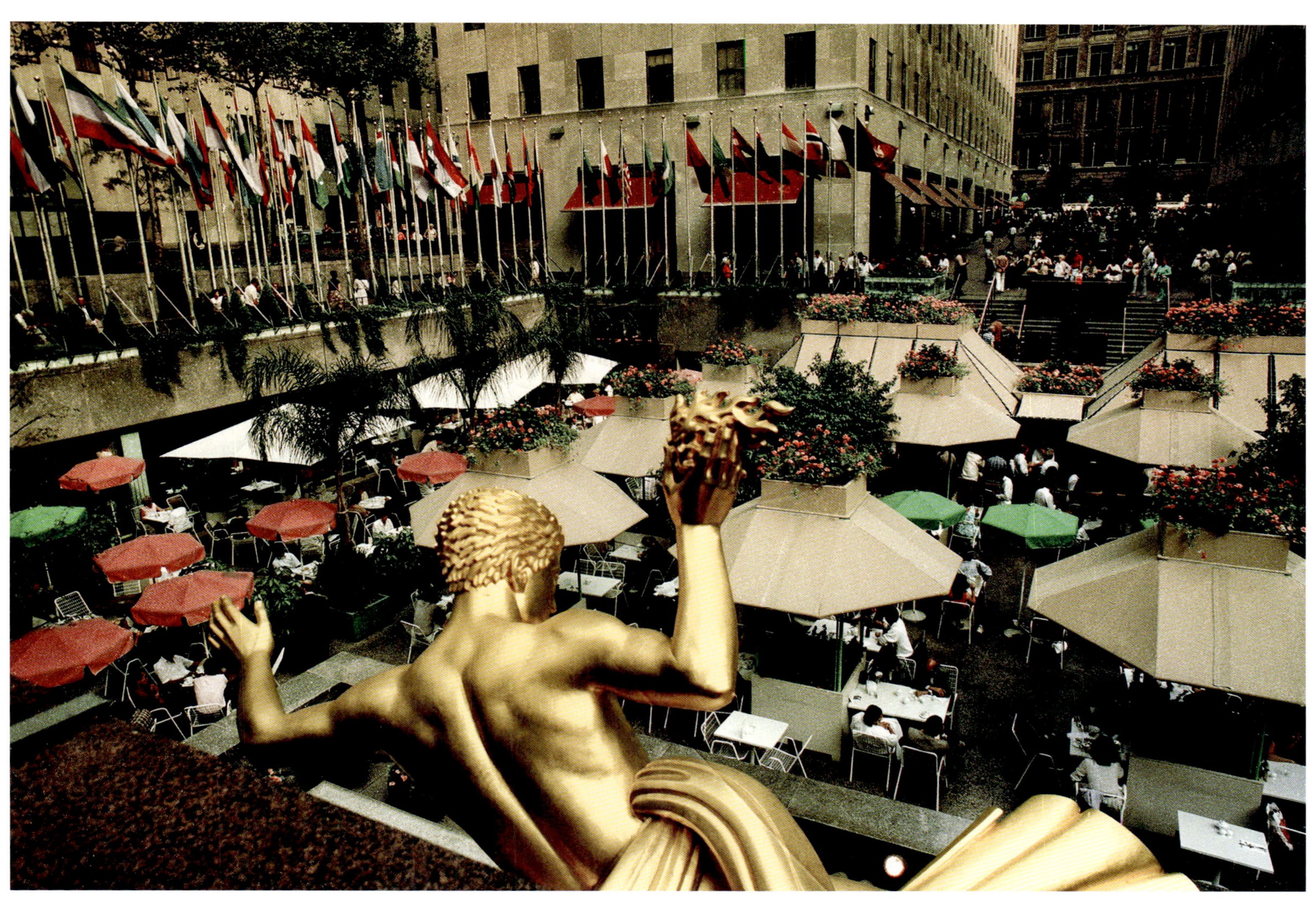

Rockefeller Center Court, Paul Manship, New York, 1985

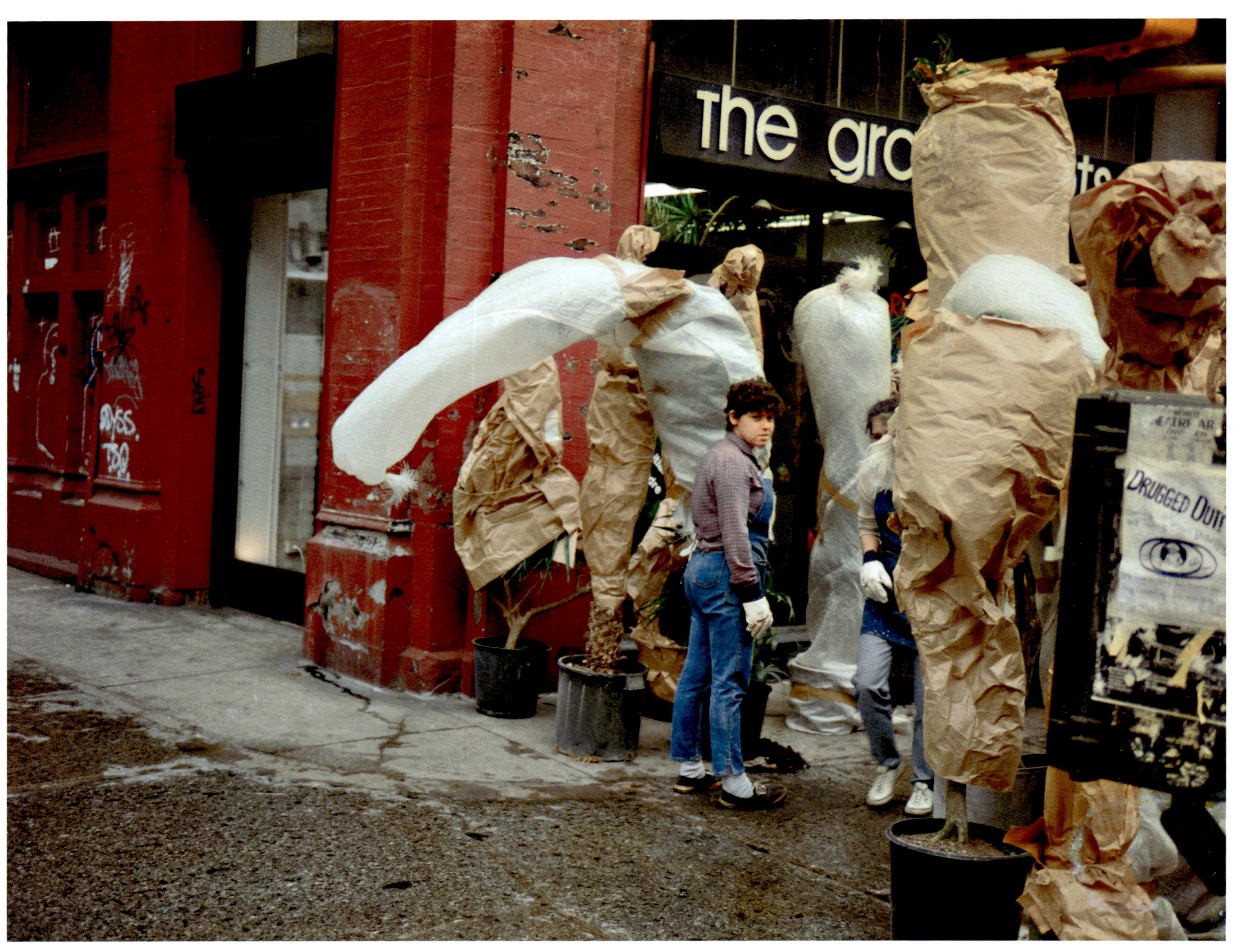

Trees Becoming Statuesque, New York, 1984

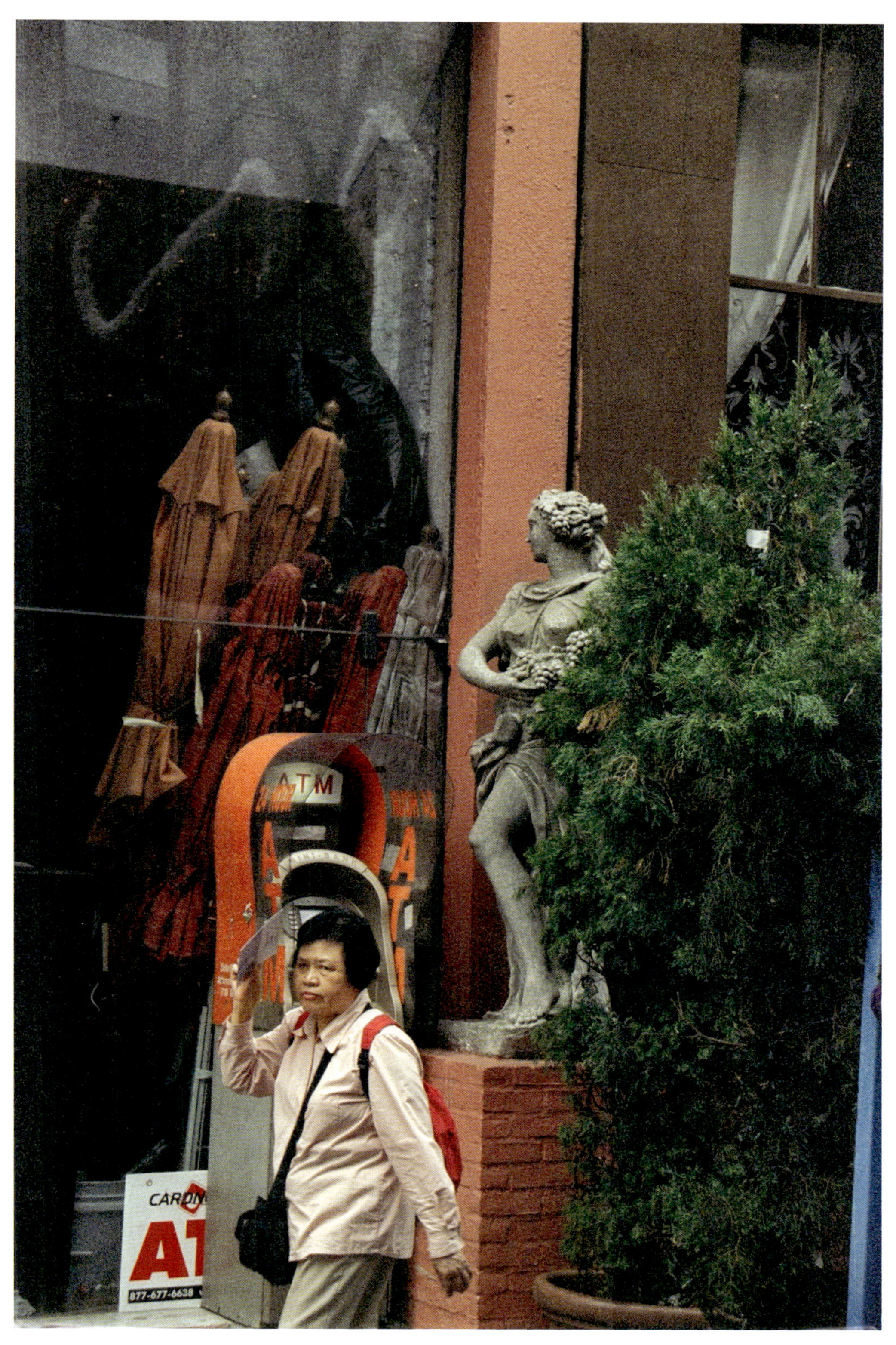

Statue, Little Italy, New York, 2013

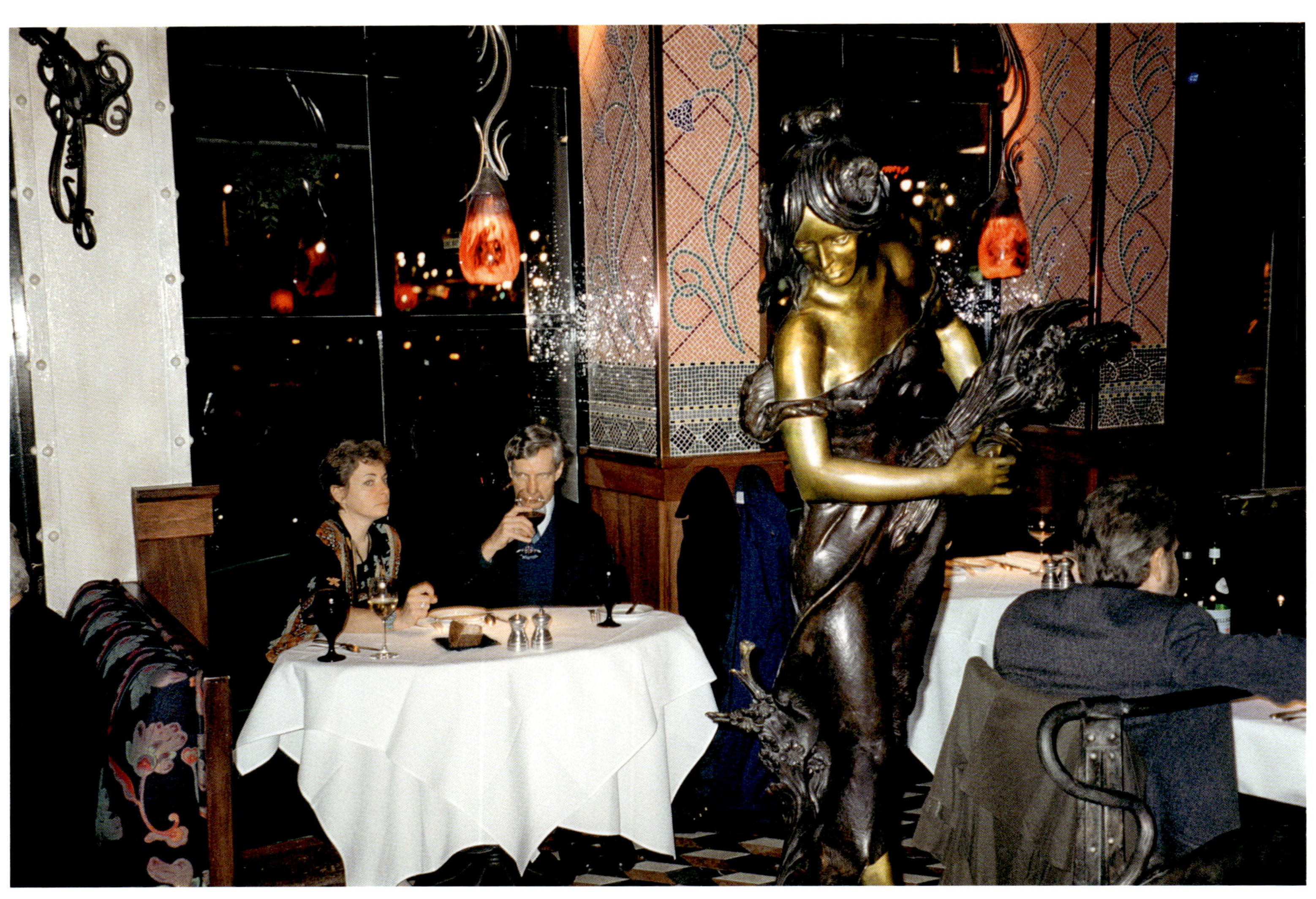

Couple in Upscale Restaurant, San Francisco, 2001

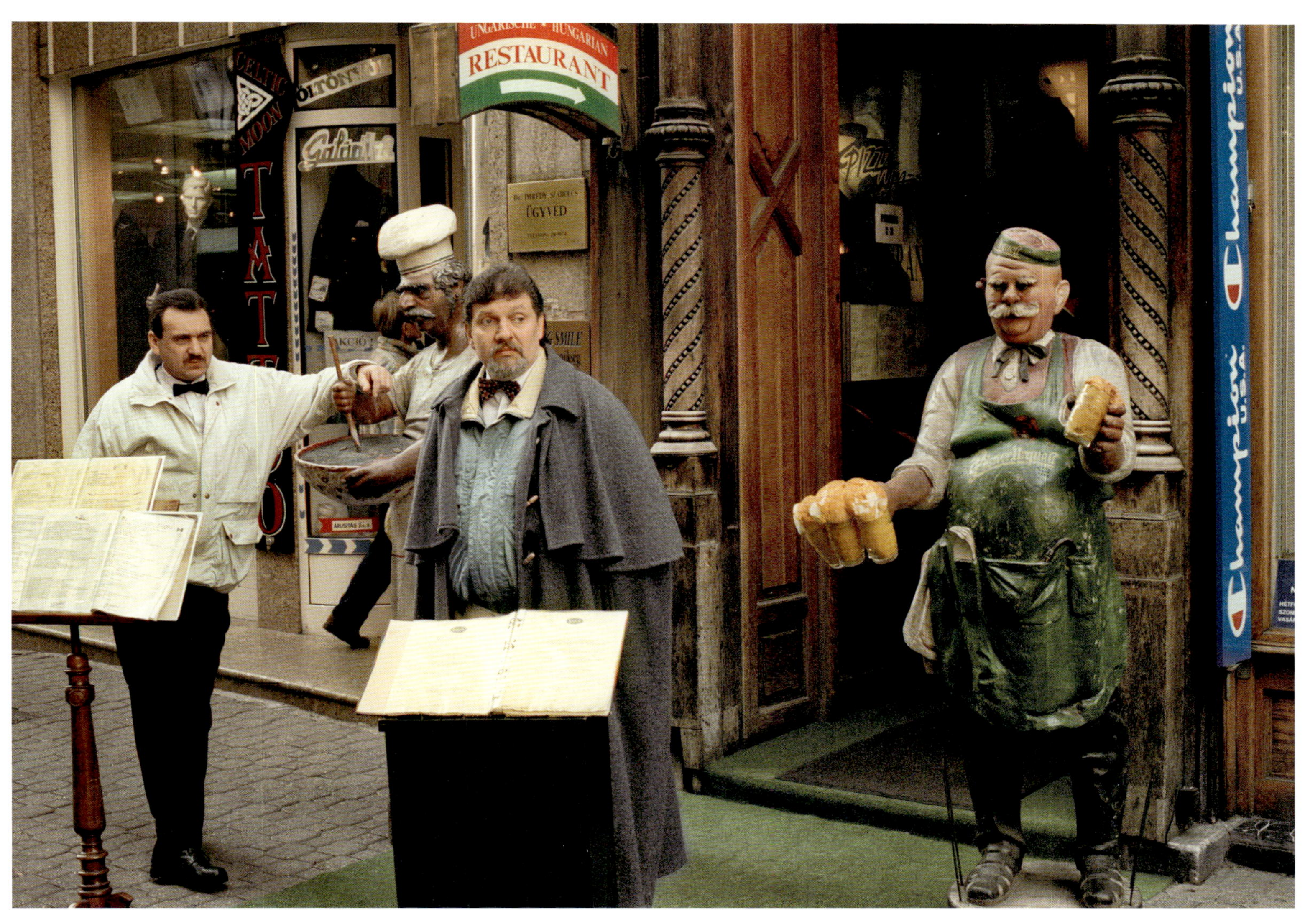

Restaurant Personnel, Budapest, 1998

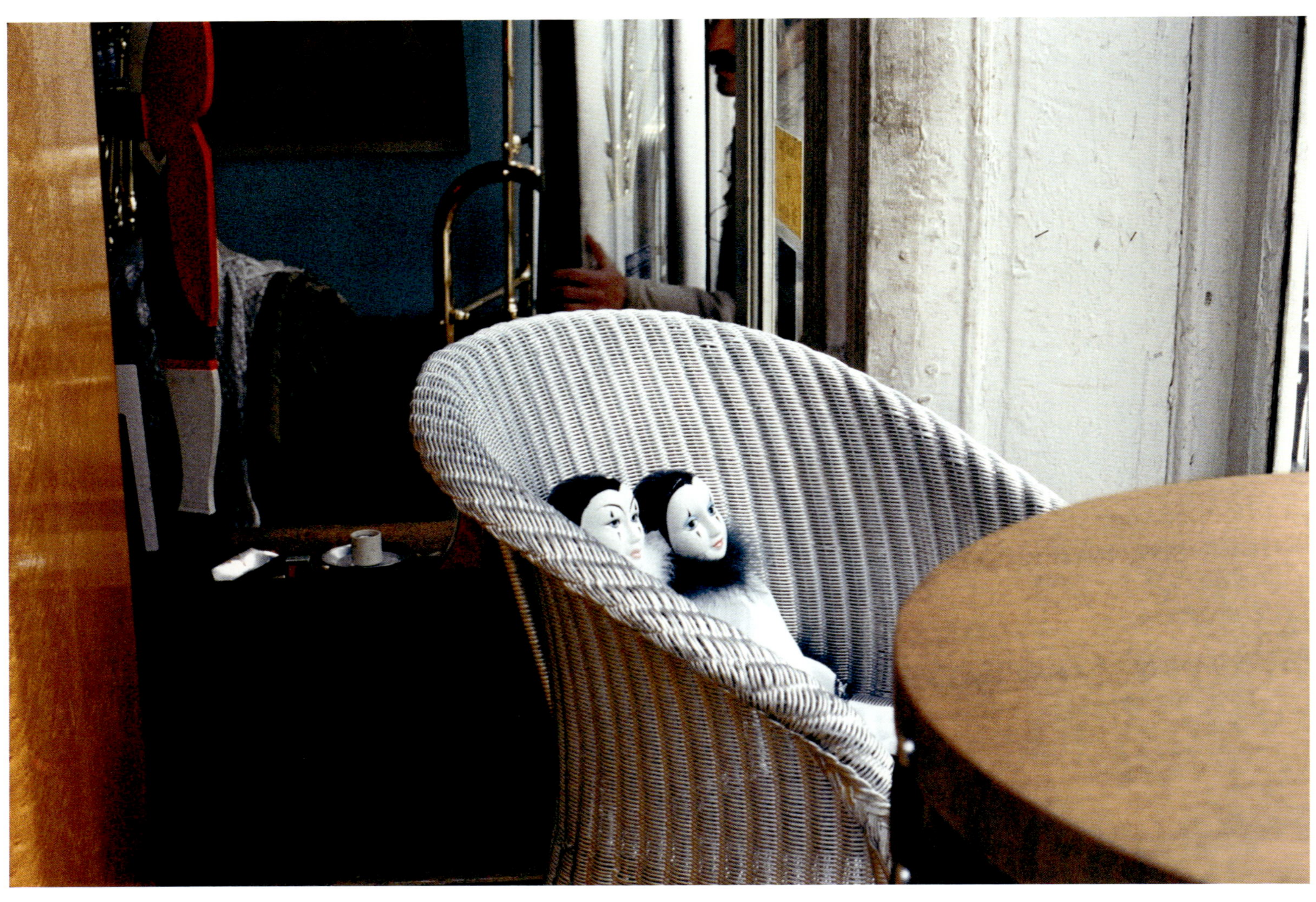

Young Cronies, New York, 2008

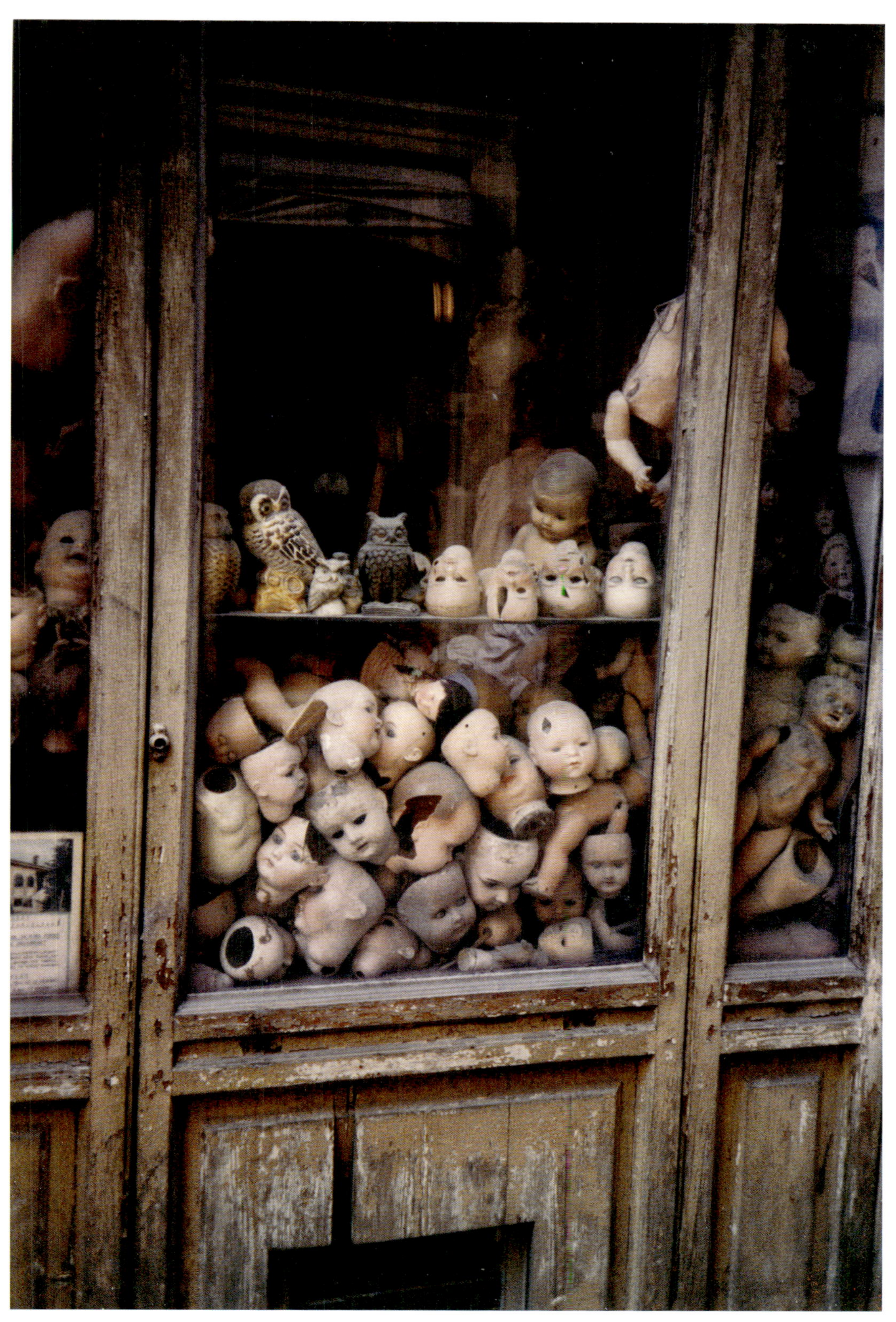

Baby Heads, near Rome, 2000

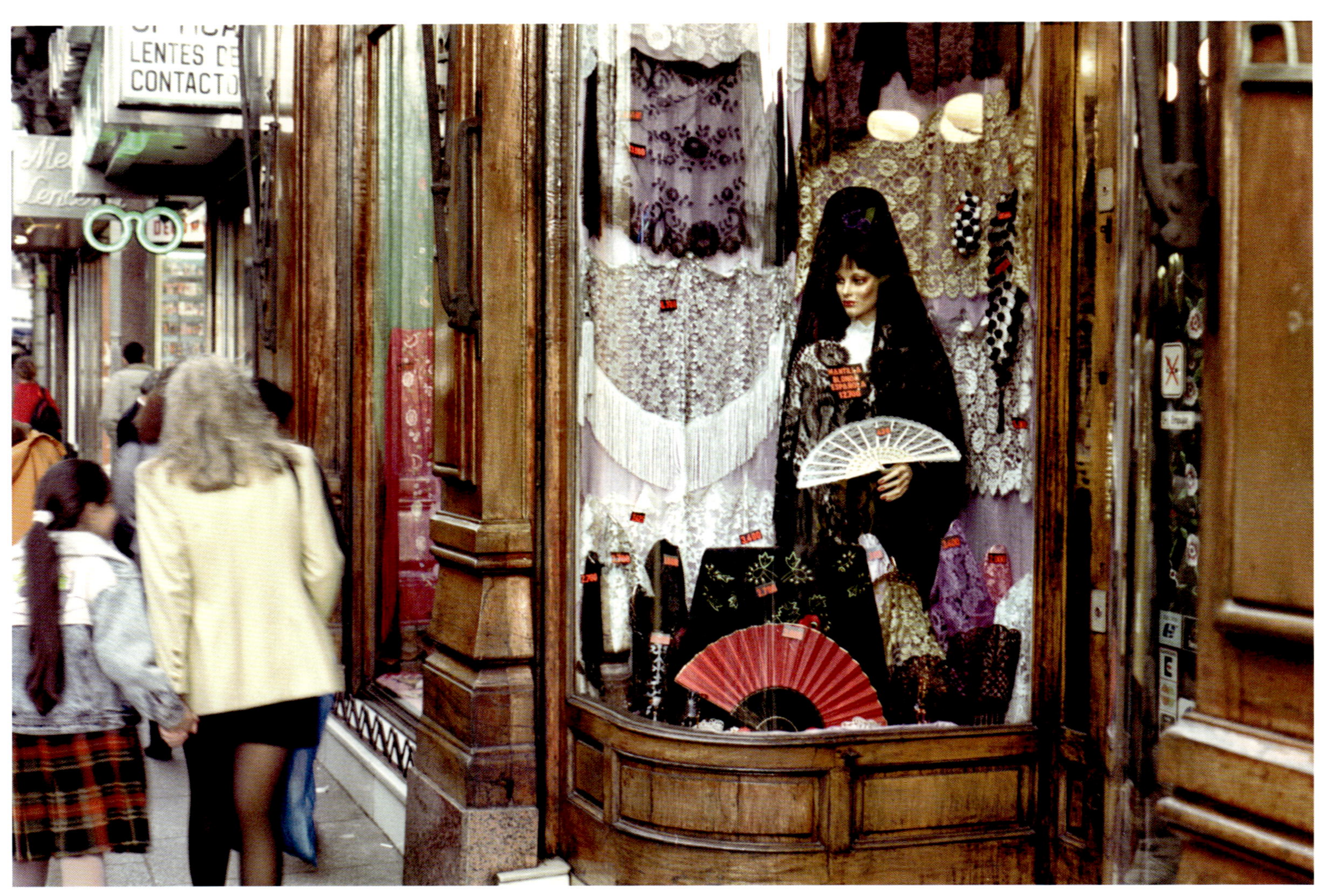

Effigy in Madrid, 1993

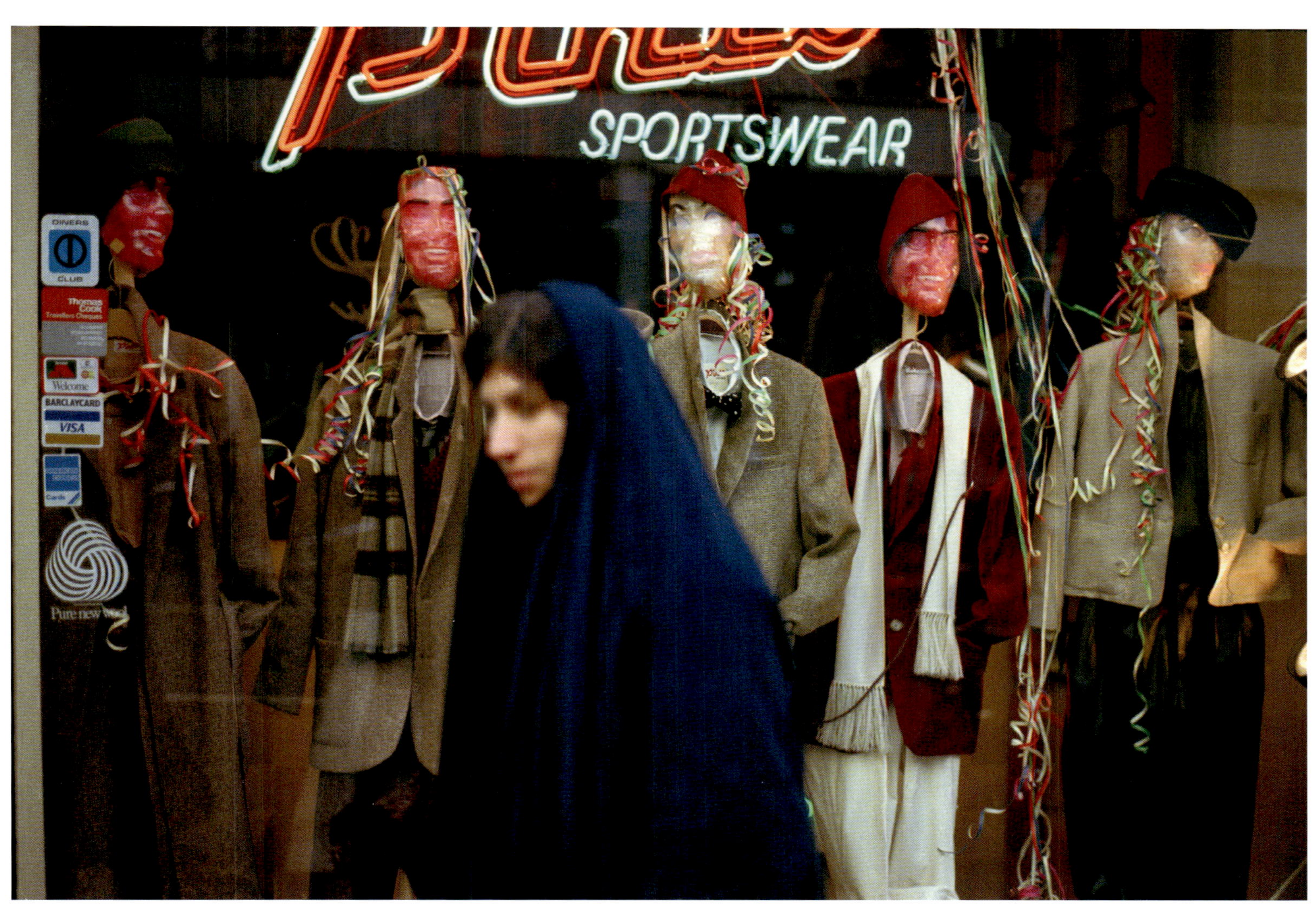

Haberdasher Window, London, 1978

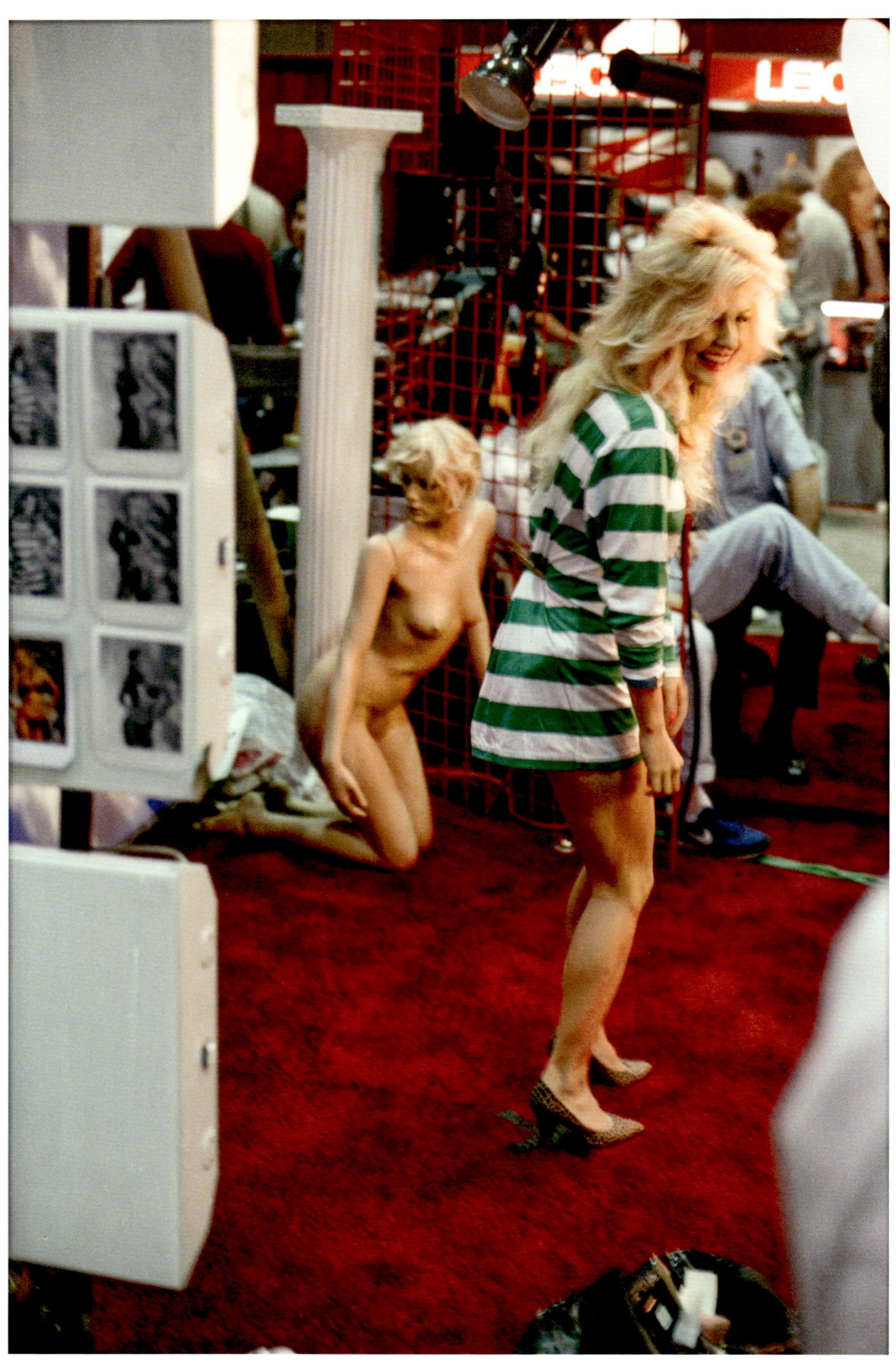

Model With Fake Nude, Los Angeles, 1994

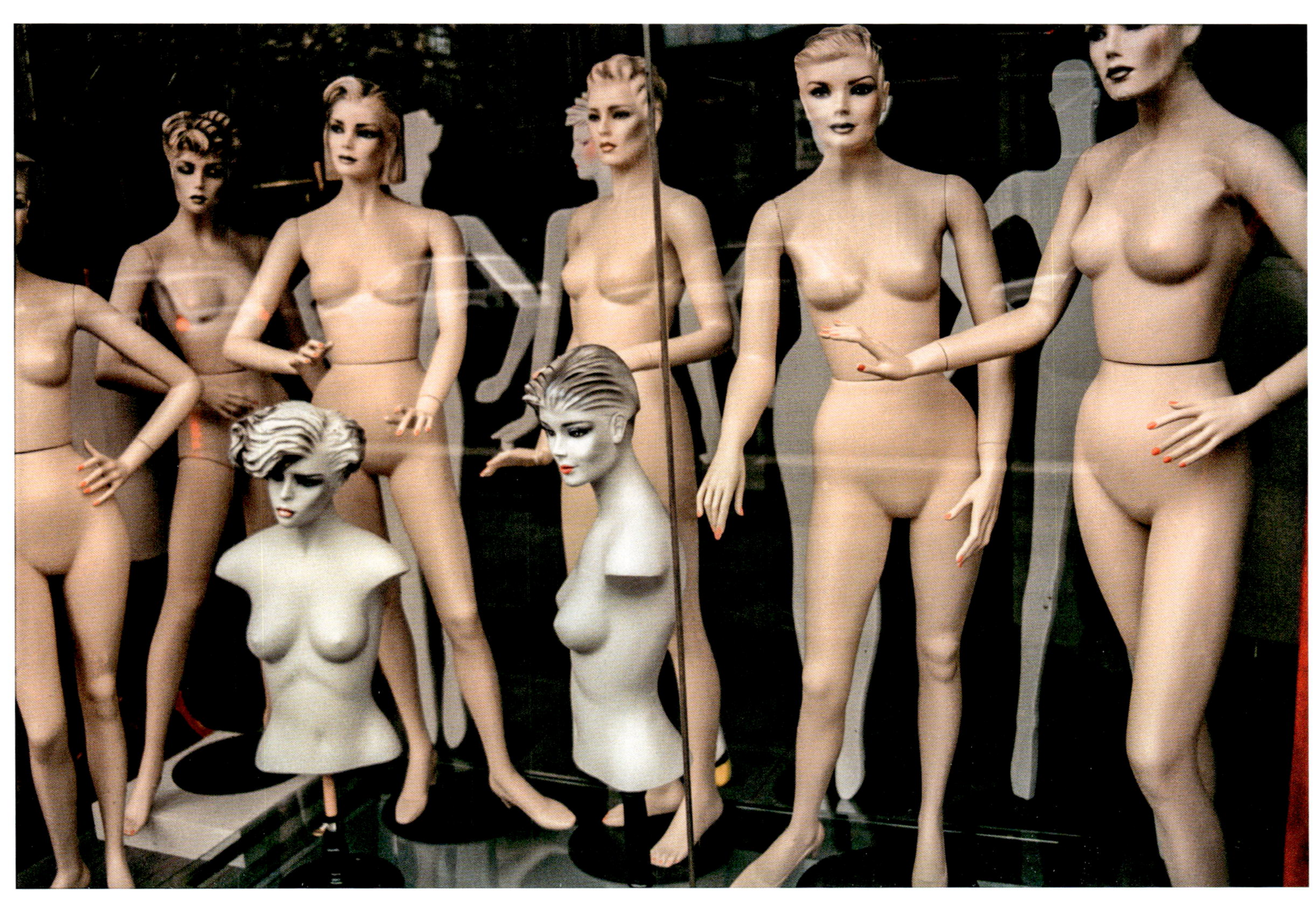

Crowd of Nude Mannequins, Los Angeles, 1989

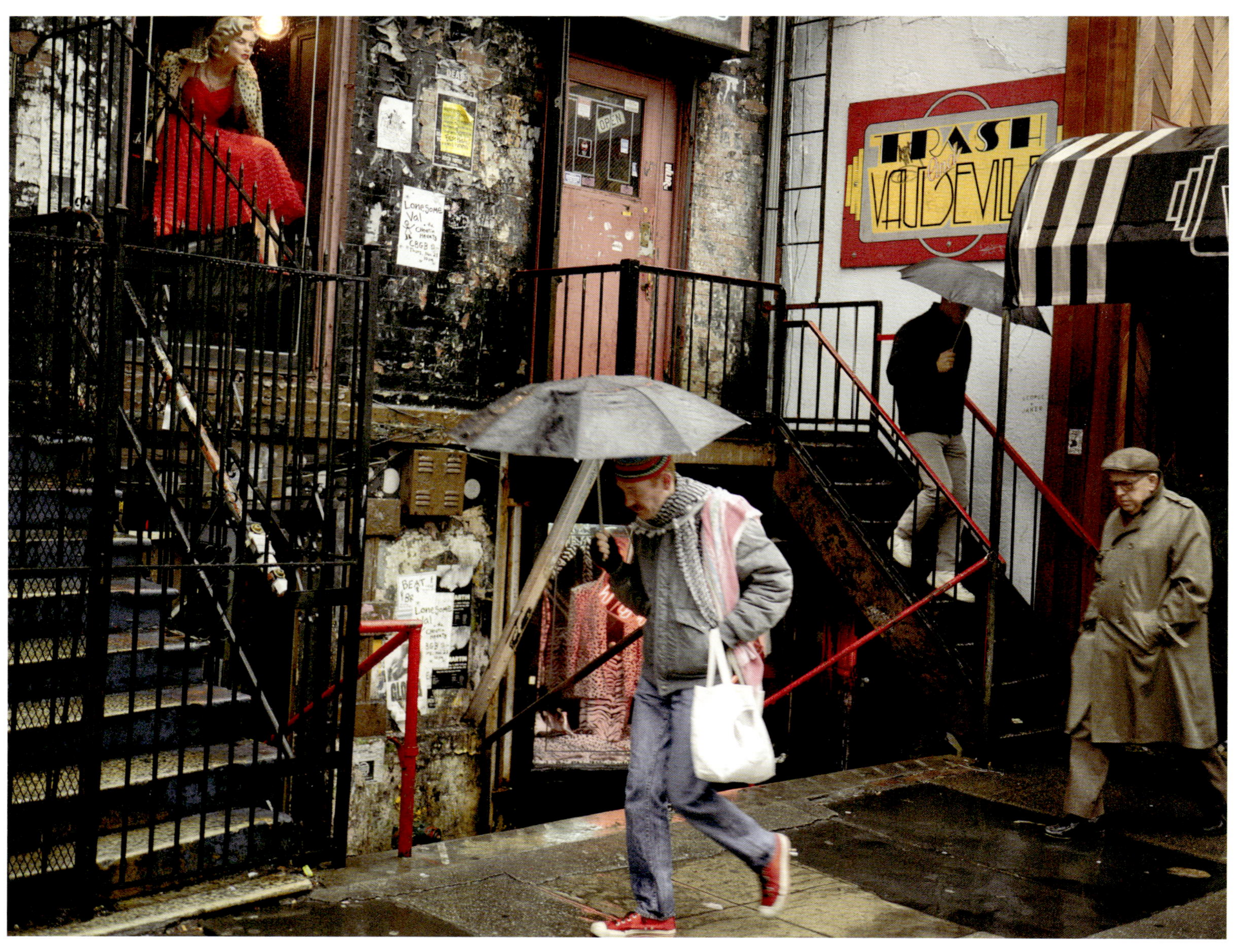

Walking in the Rain, The Red Sneakers, St. Mark's Place, New York, 1985

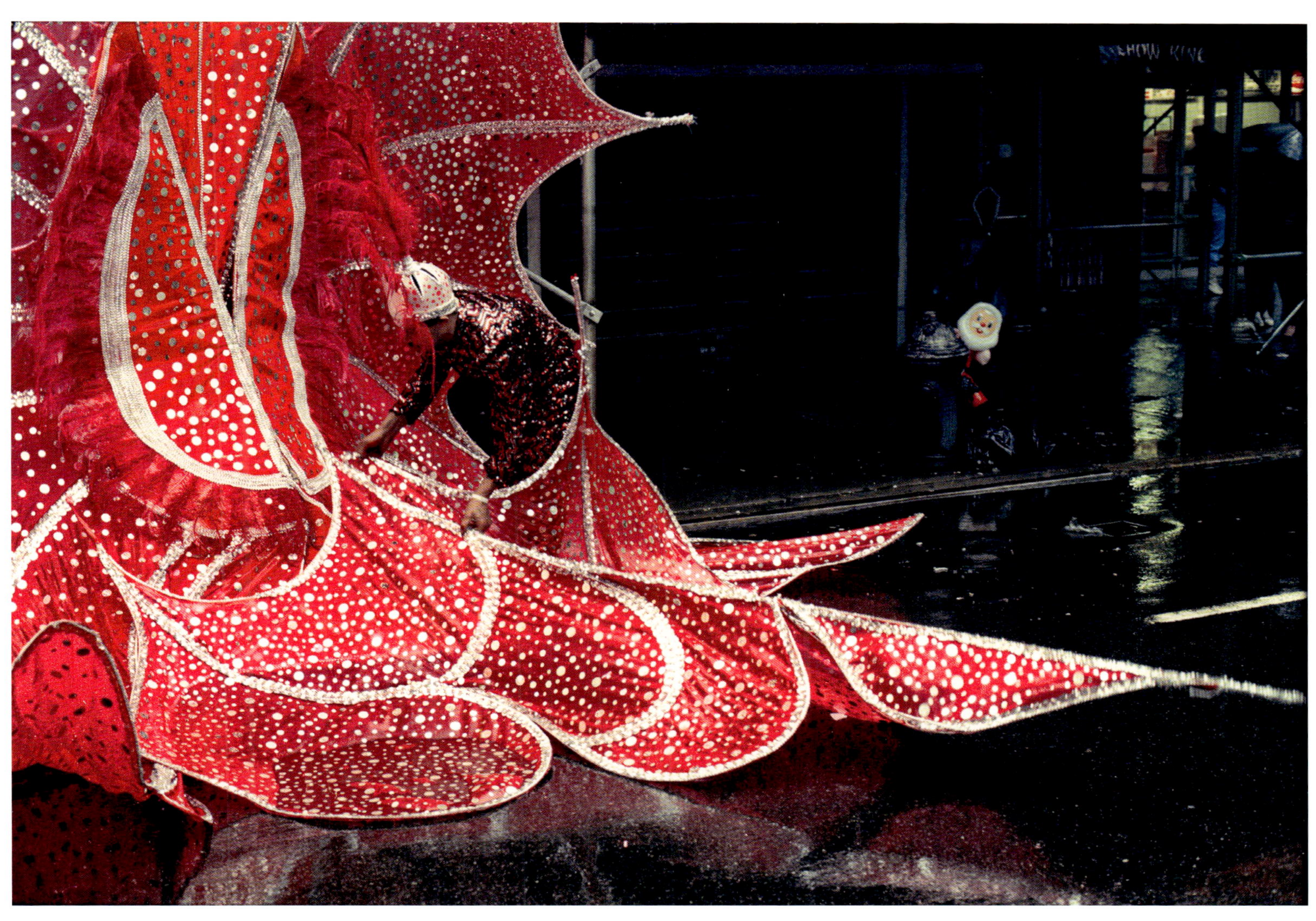

Little Santa, November Macy's Parade, New York, 1993

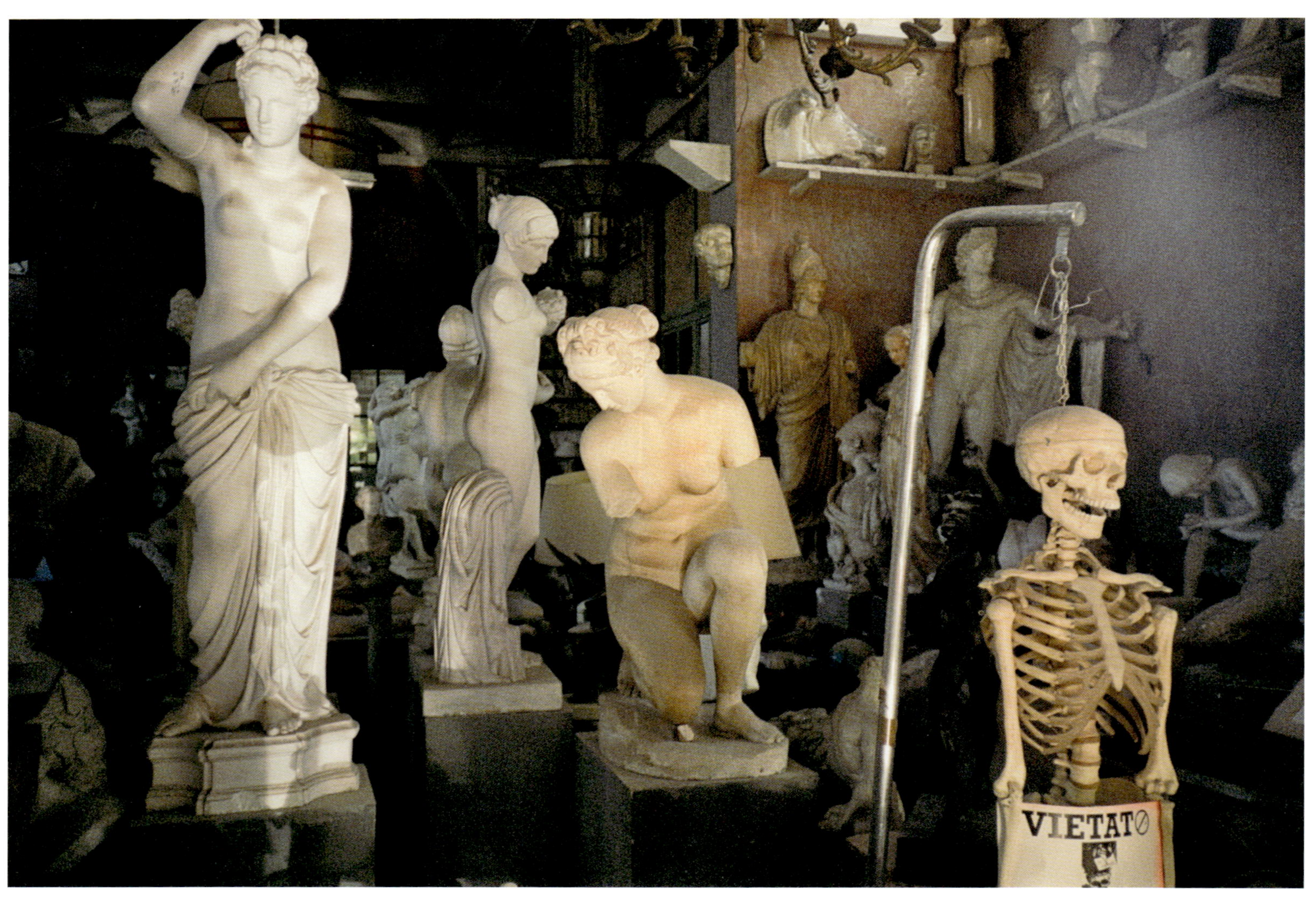

Studio Antiquities with Skeleton, Cinecittá Rome, 2000

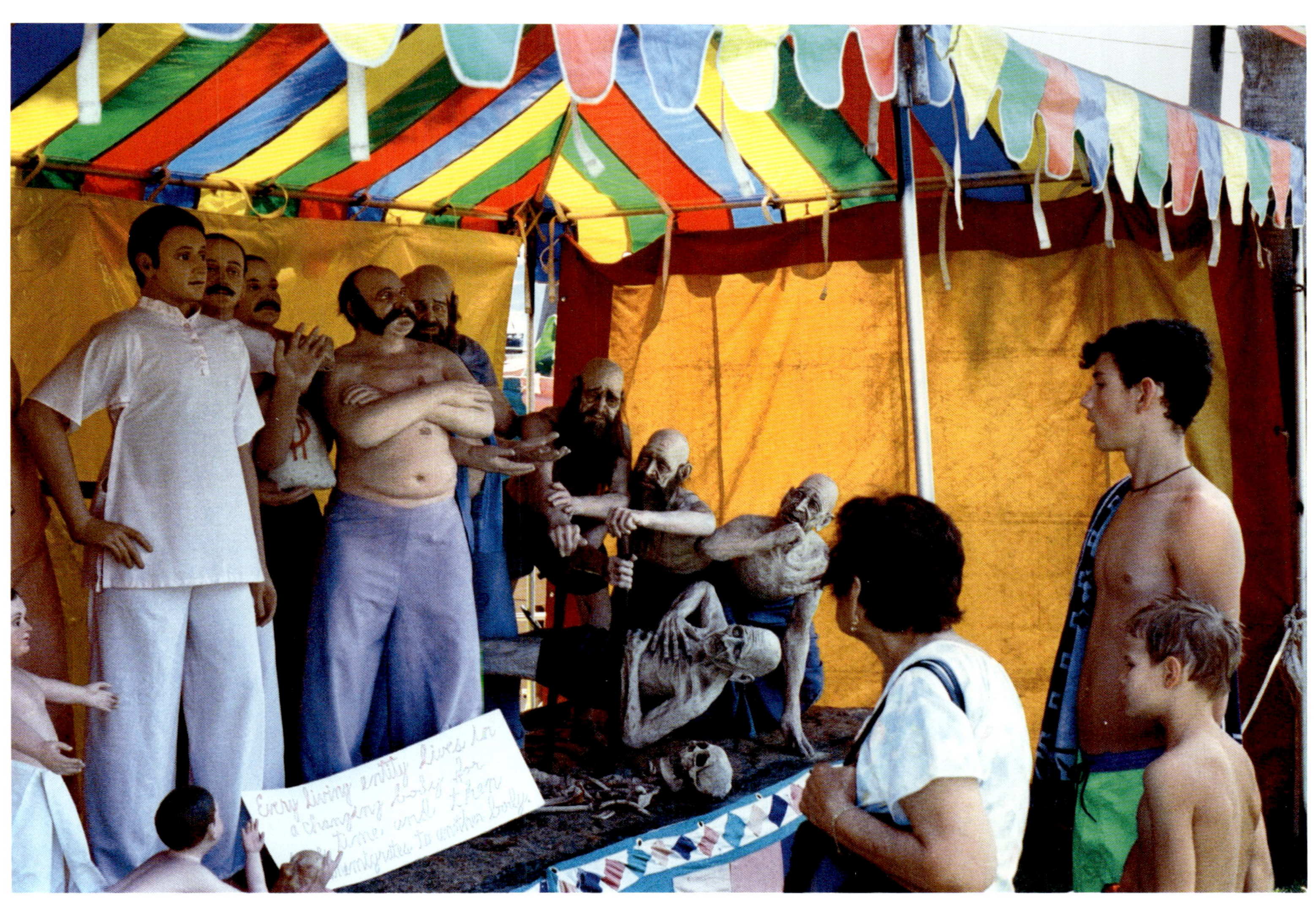

Hare Krishna Display, Los Angeles, 1994

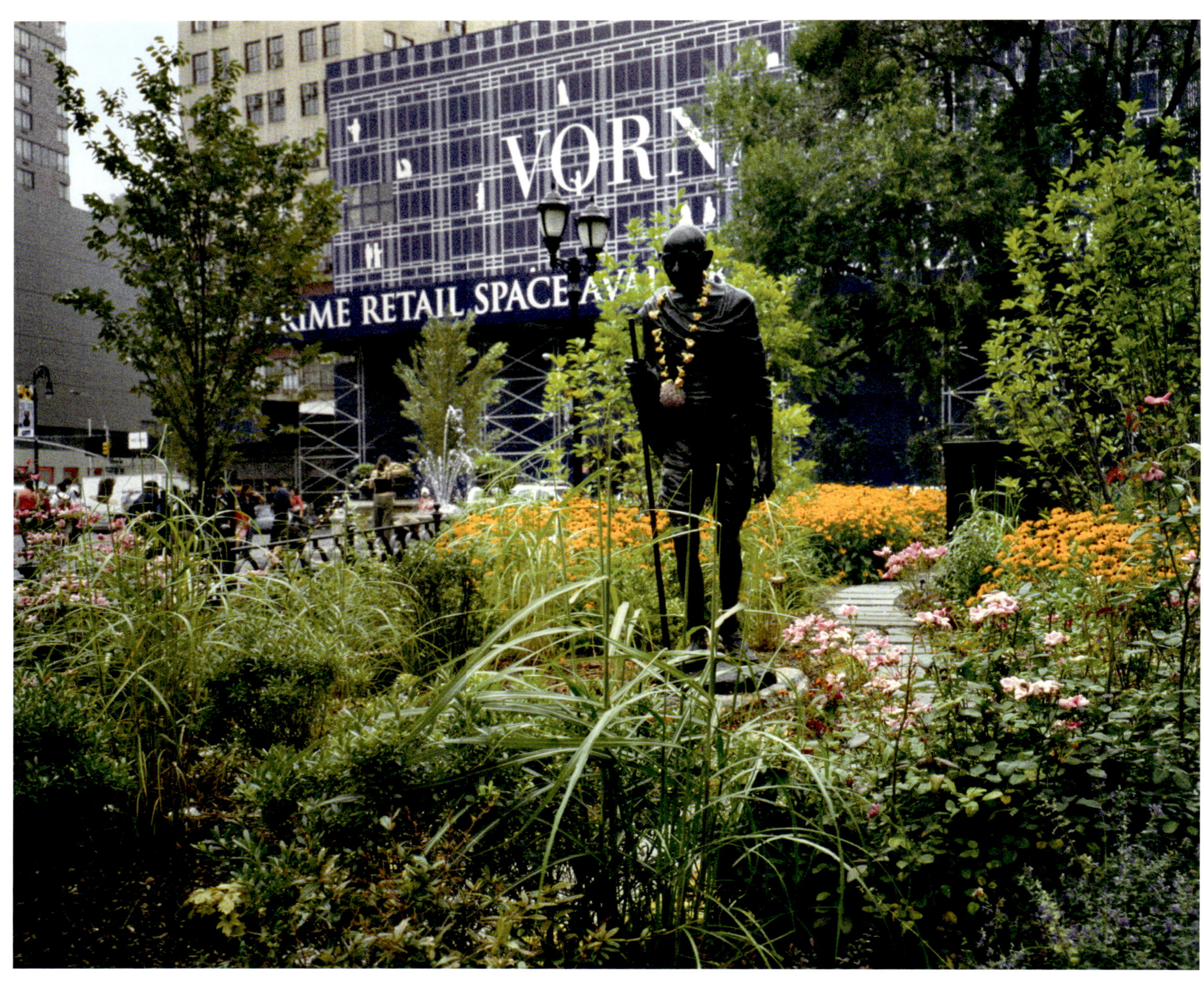

Gandhi Presiding Over Union Square, New York, 2001

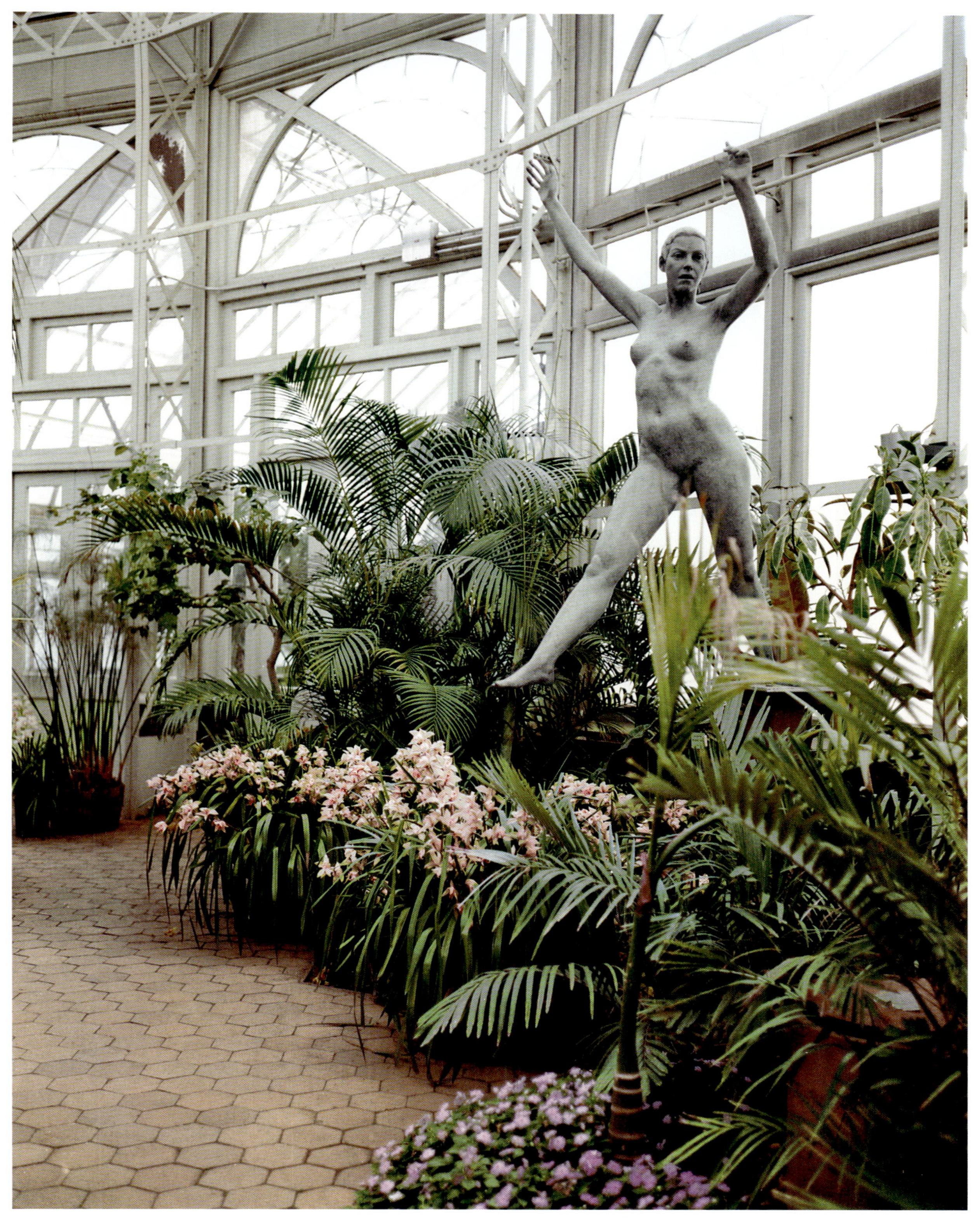

Jubilant Statue in the Bronx Botanical Garden, New York, 1981

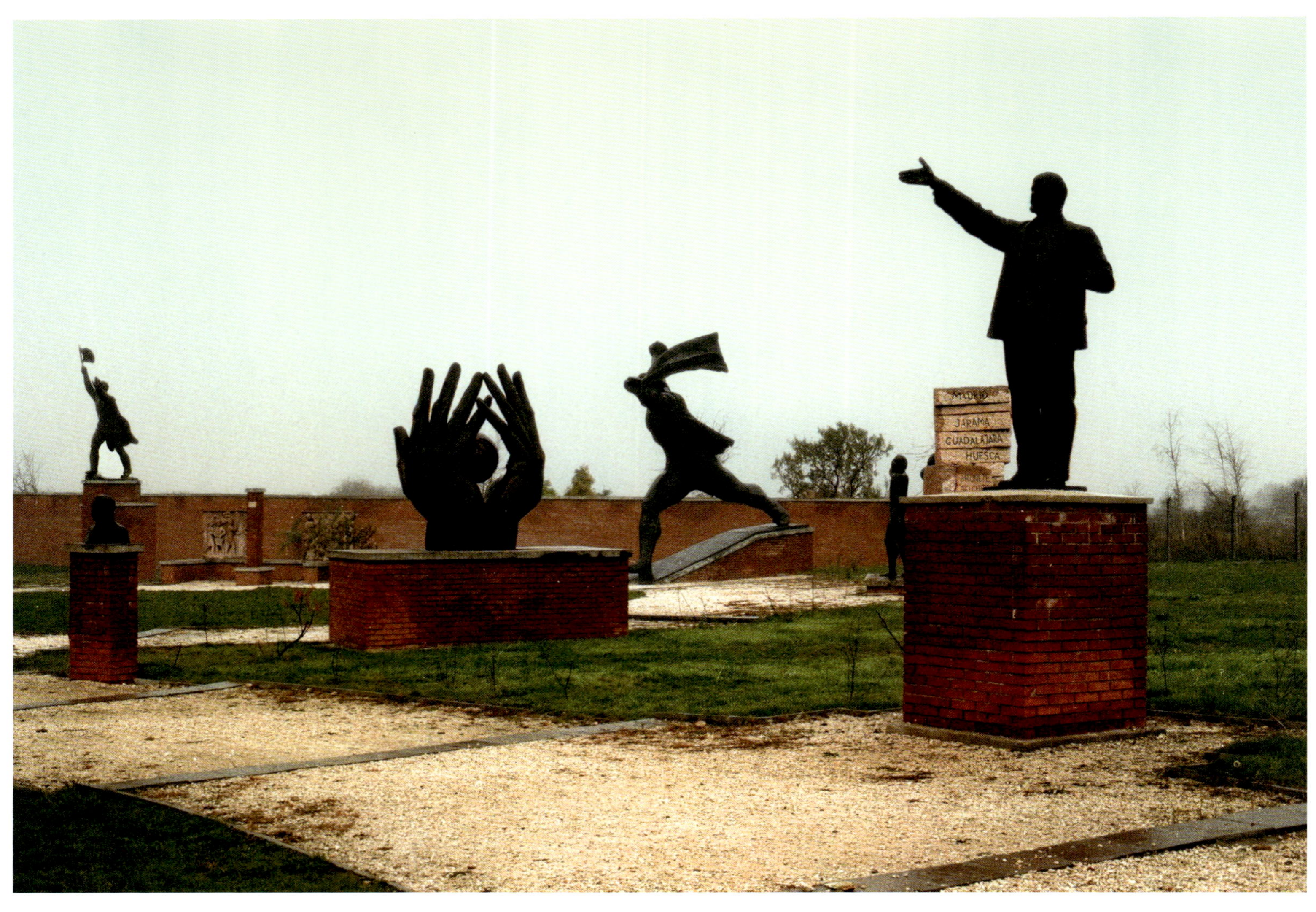

Socialist Realist Sculpture, Budapest, 1978

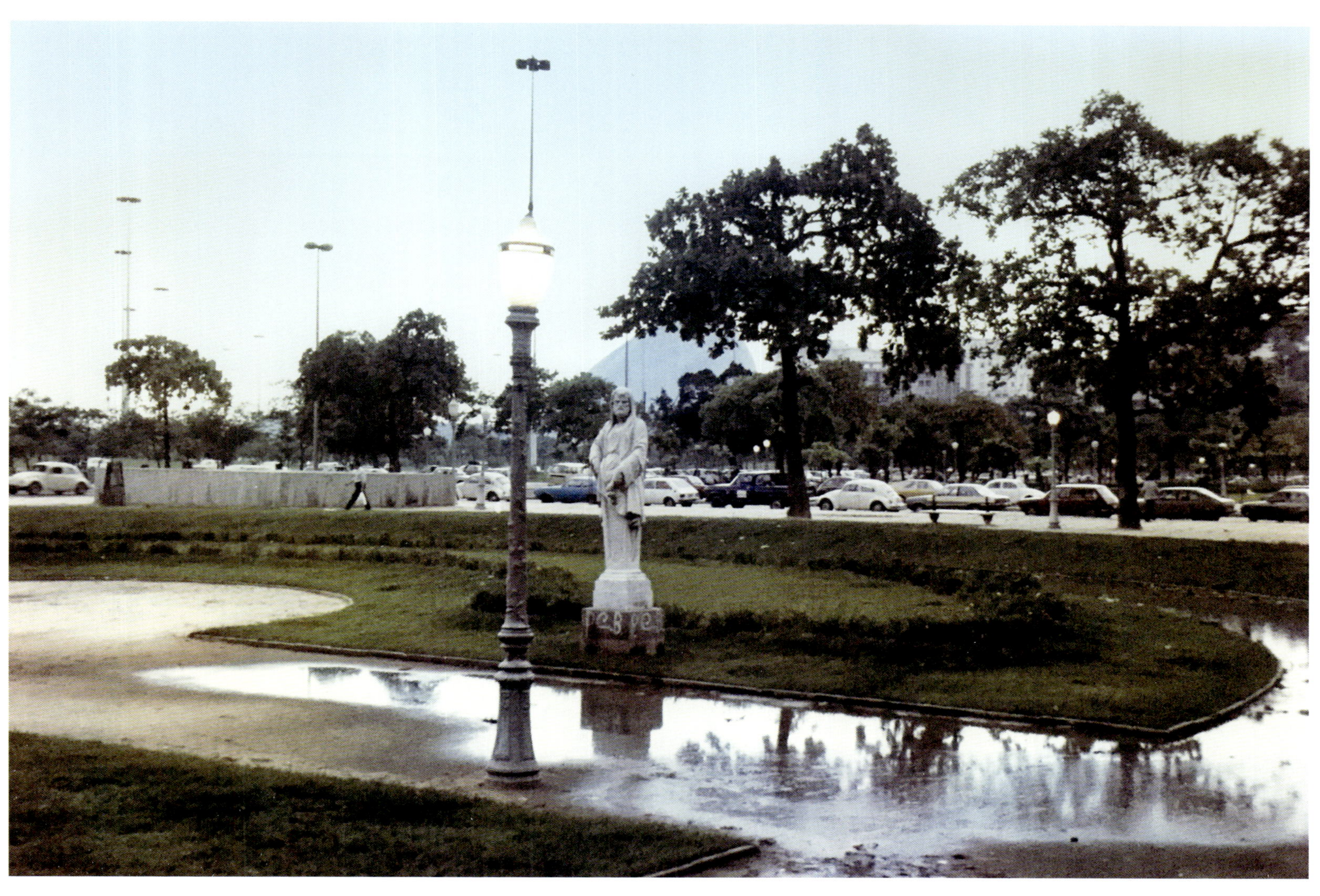

Solitary Statue, Early Morning, Rio de Janeiro, 1980

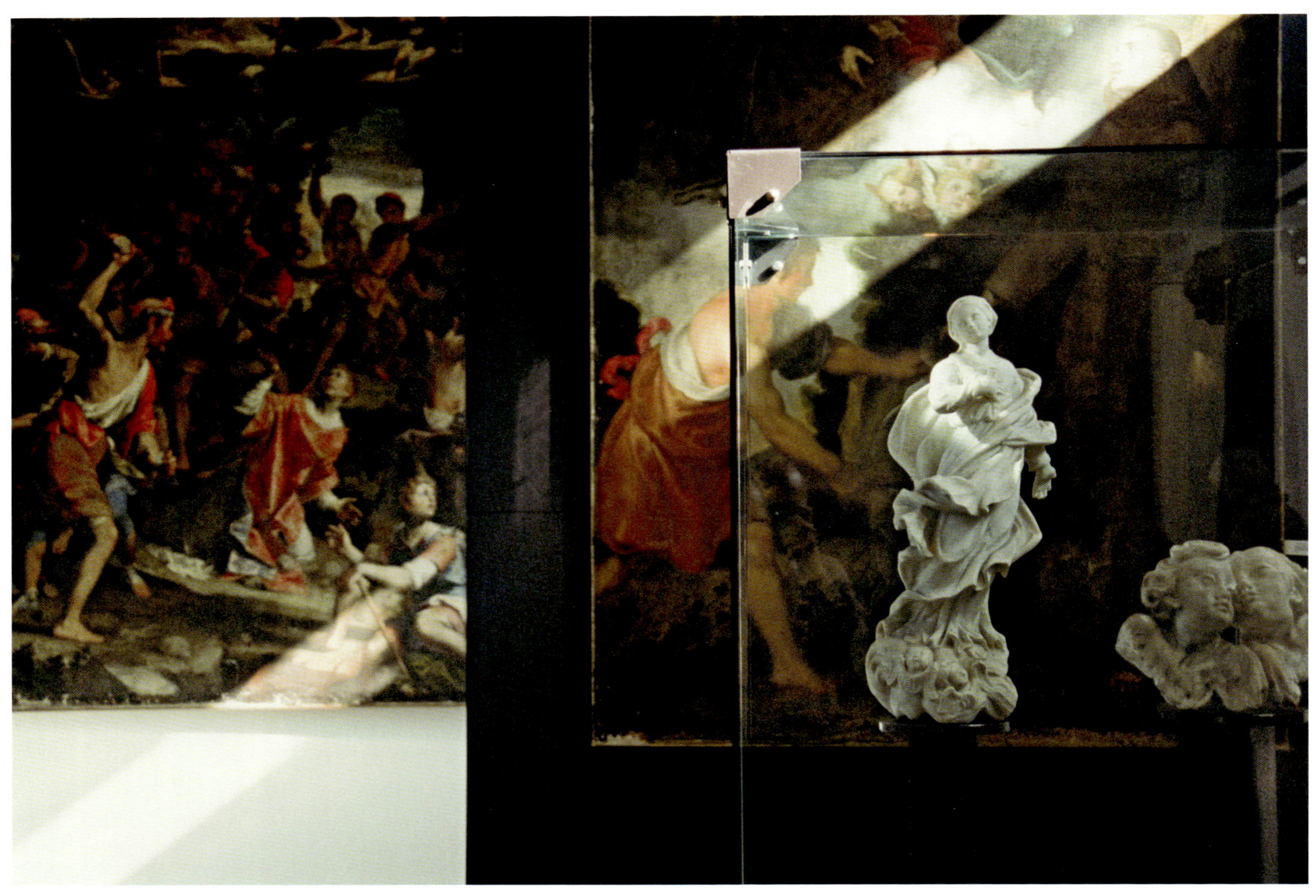

Museo Sant'Agostino, Genoa, 2001

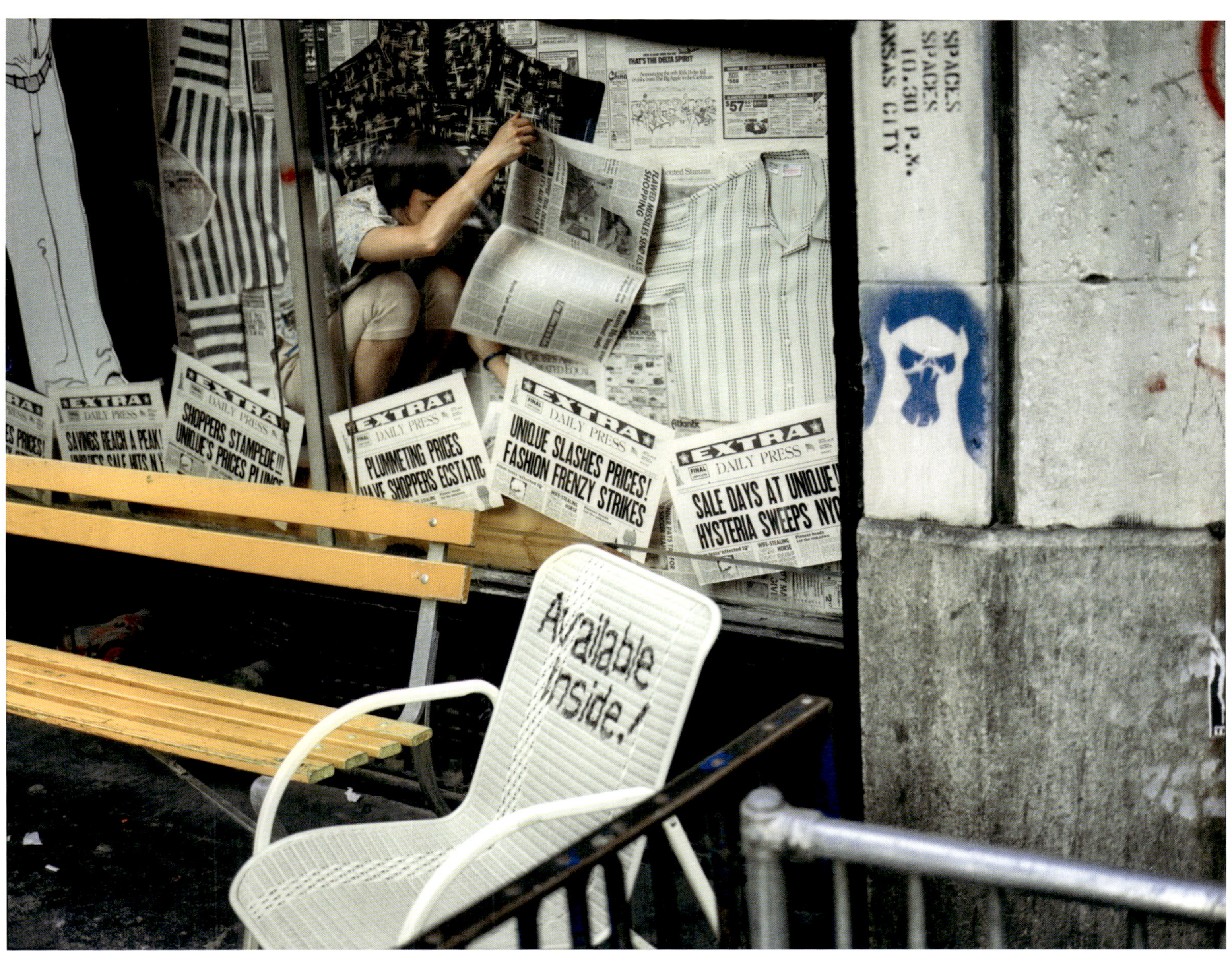

Store Window "Available Inside," New York, 1984

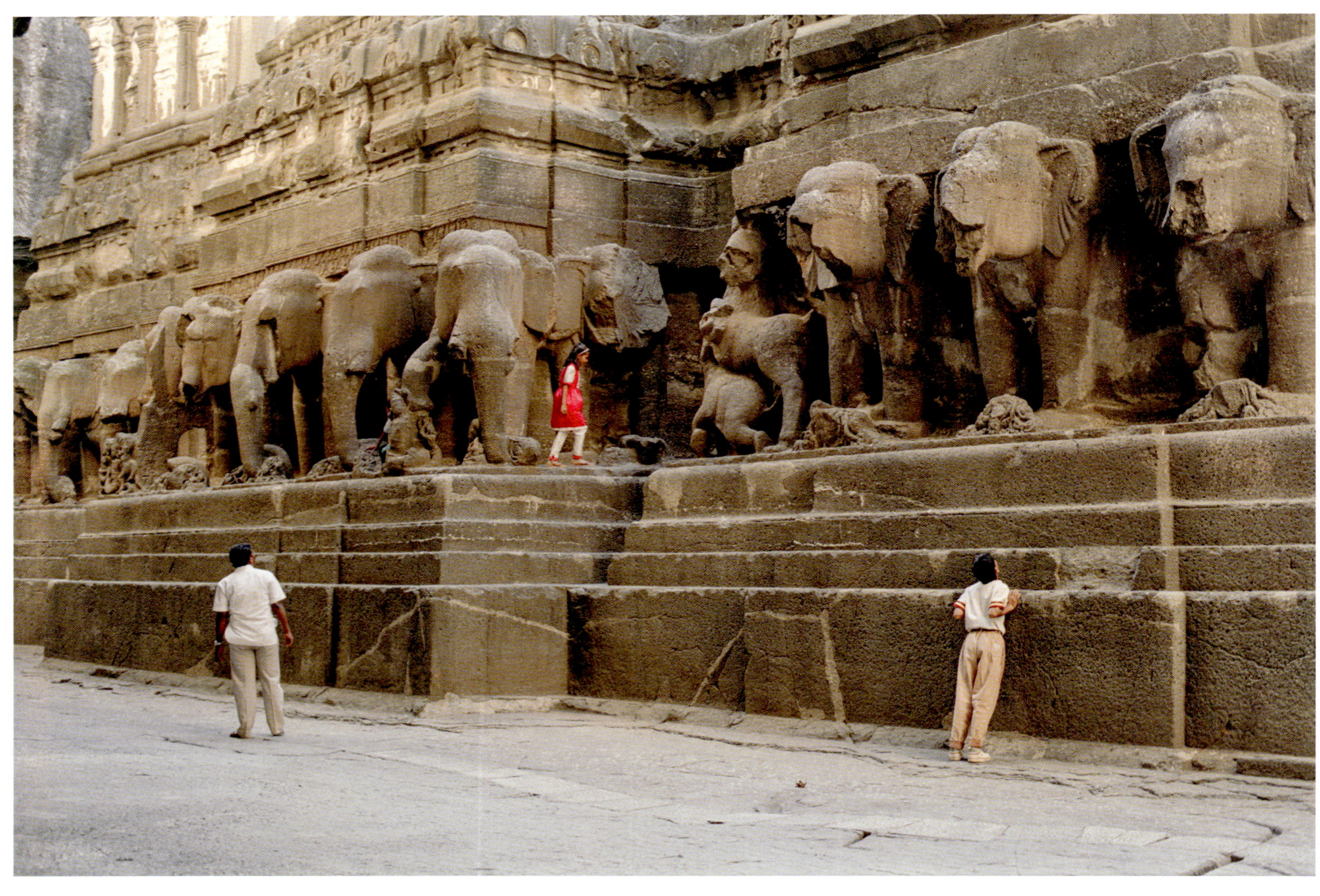

Sacred Elephants at the Ellora Caves, India, 1996

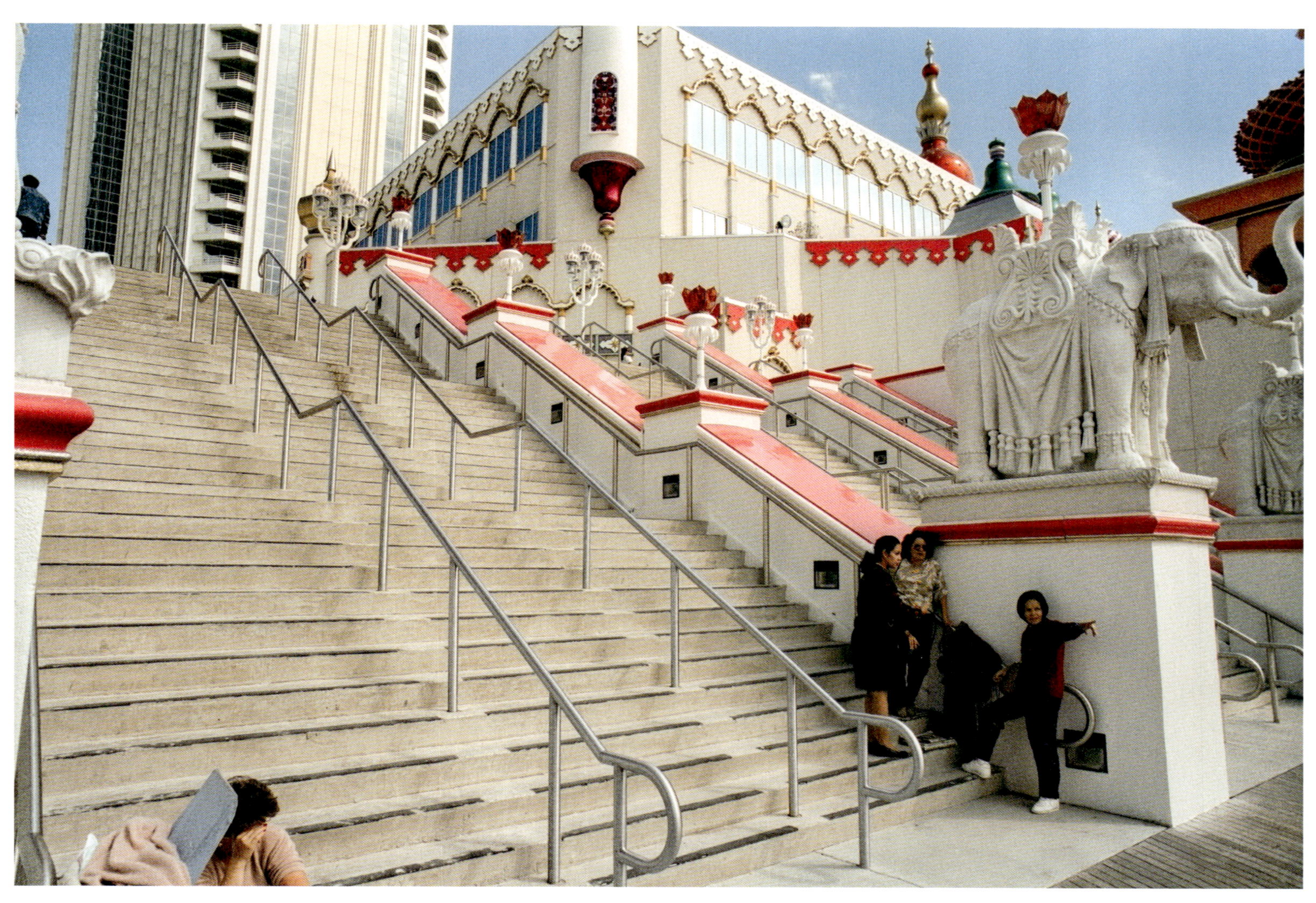

Elephant, Atlantic City, 1990

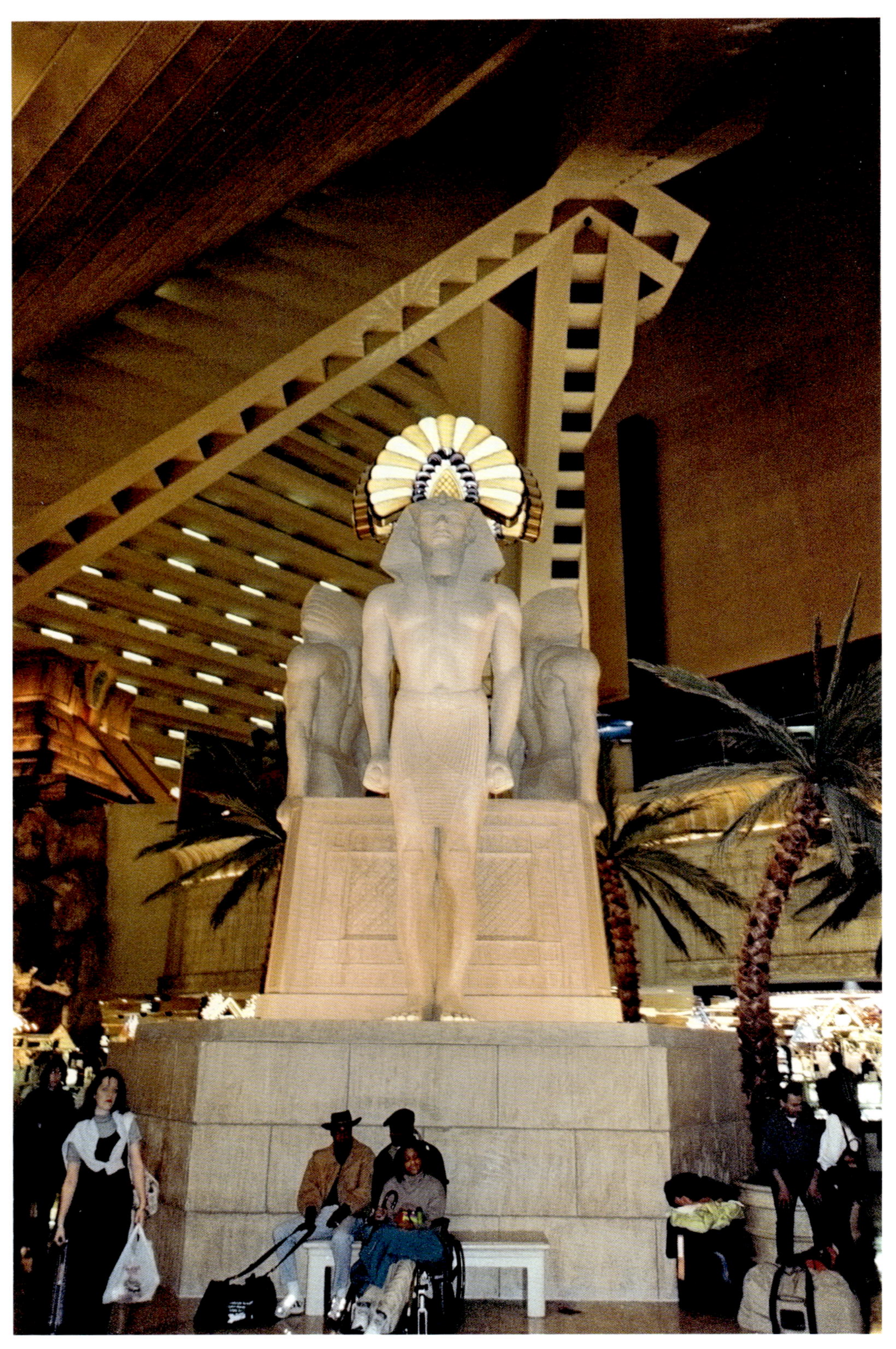

Egyptian Razzmatazz, Las Vegas, 1999

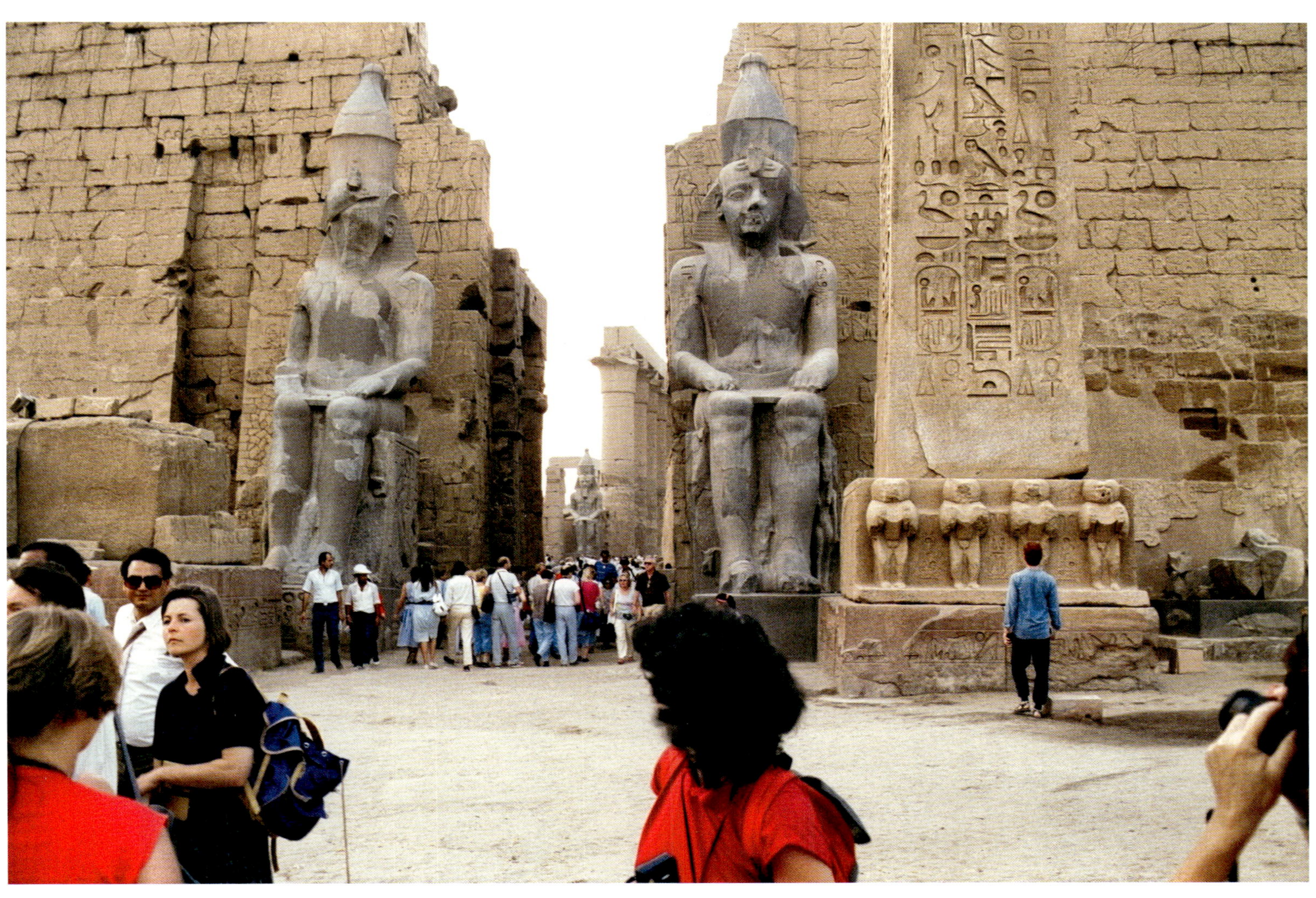

Big Shots at Karnak, Egypt, 1992

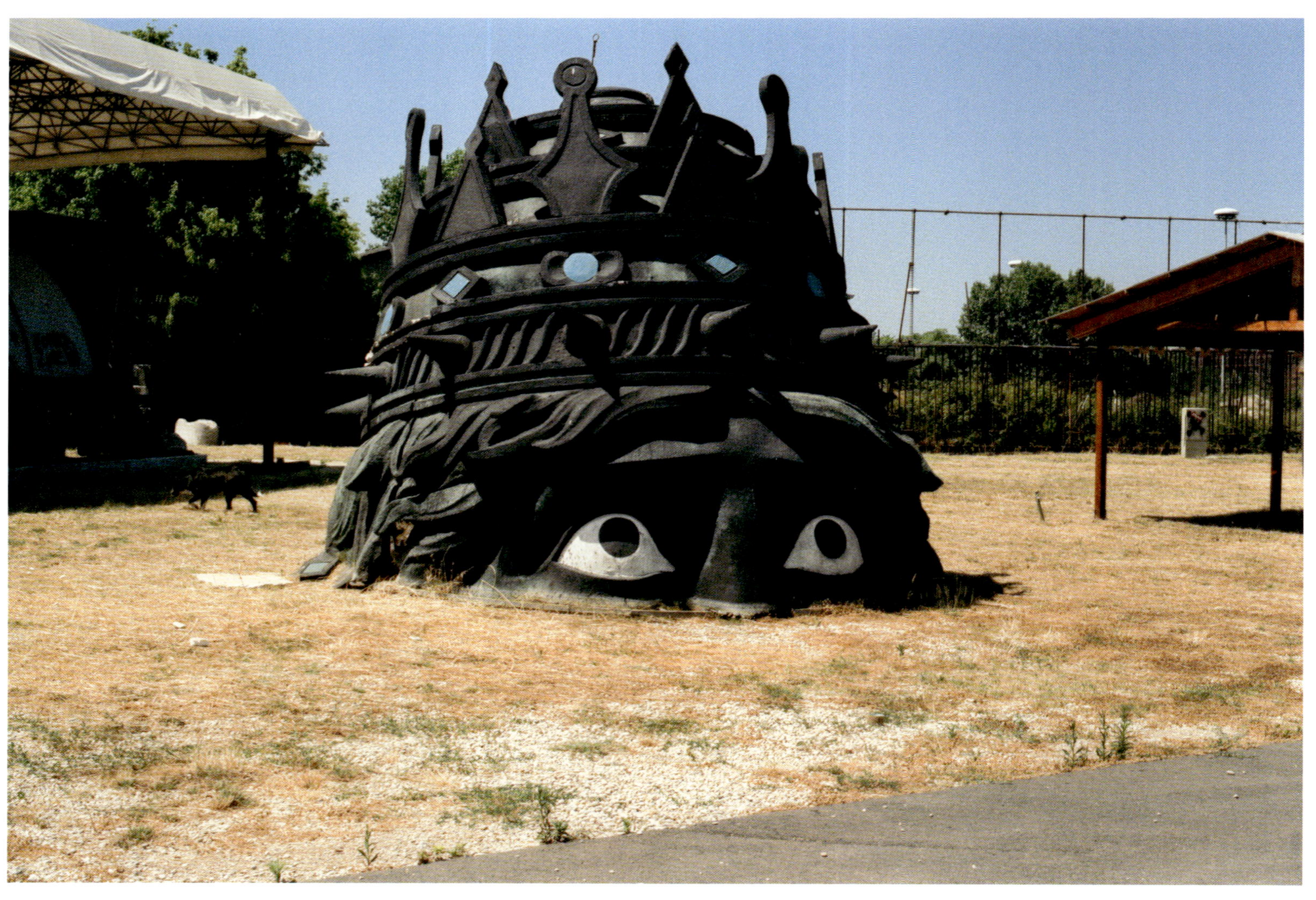

Fairy Tale Statue (Venusia Cinecittá), Rome, 2000

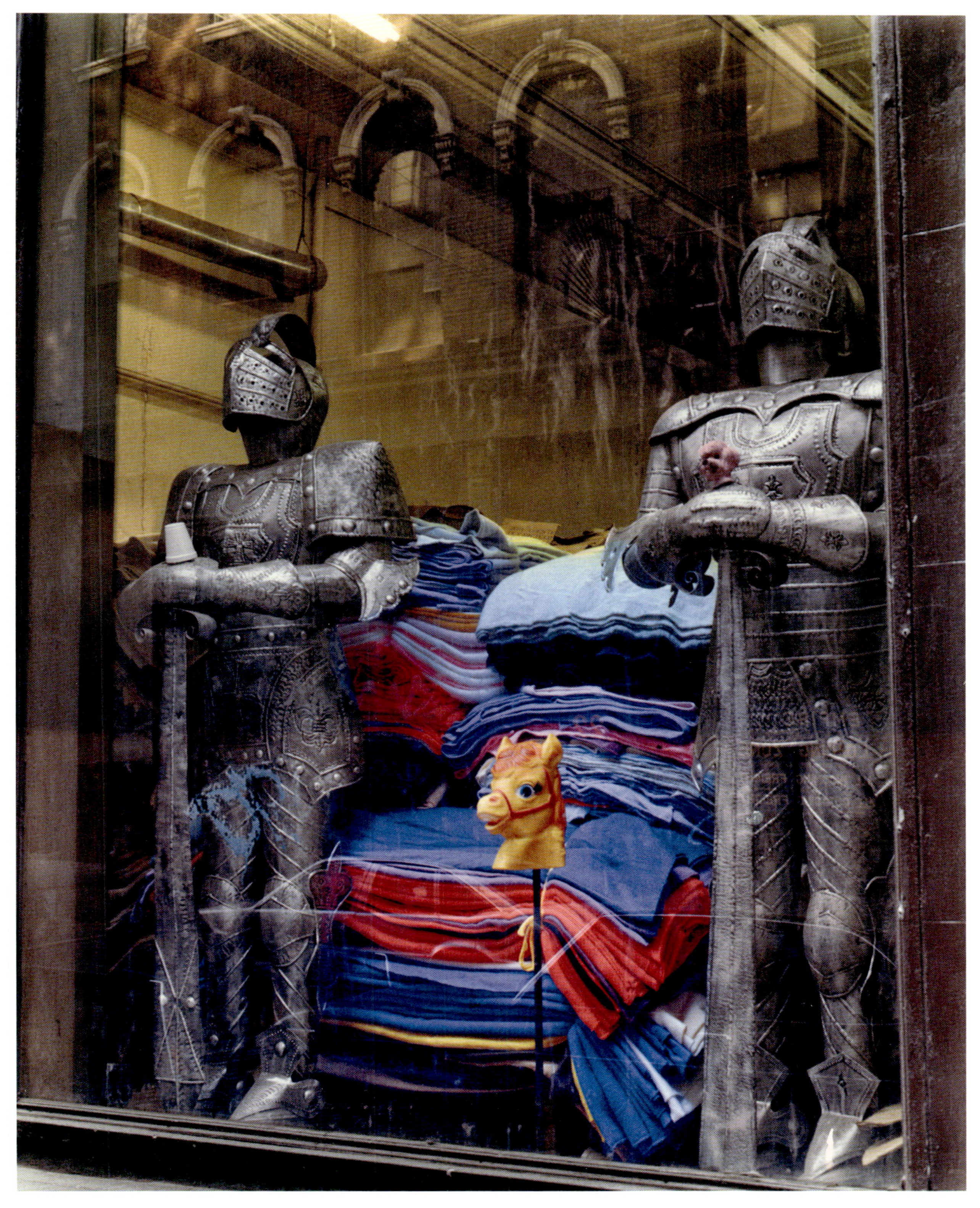

House of Piles, Broadway, New York, date unknown

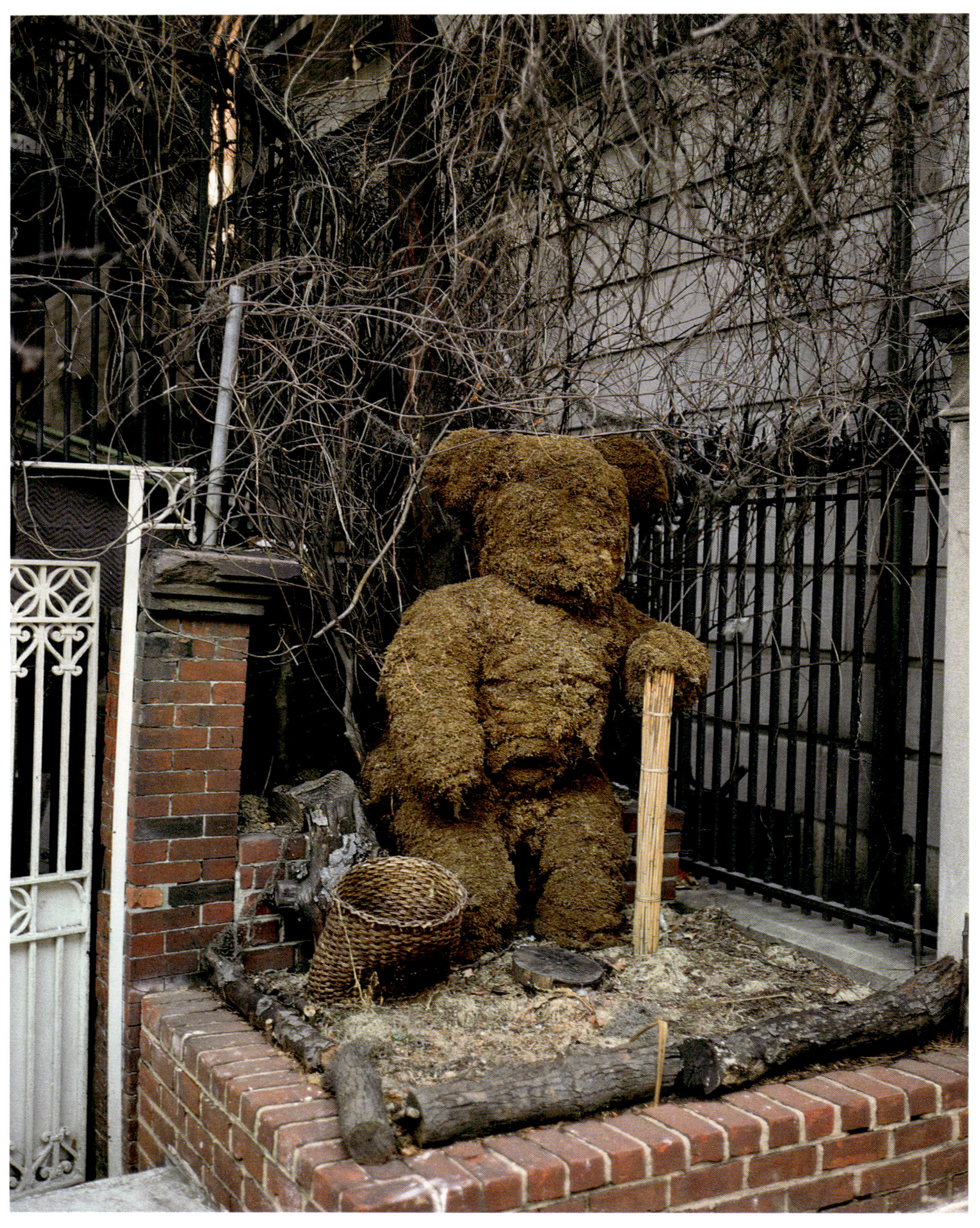

Topiary Mouse, New York, 1984

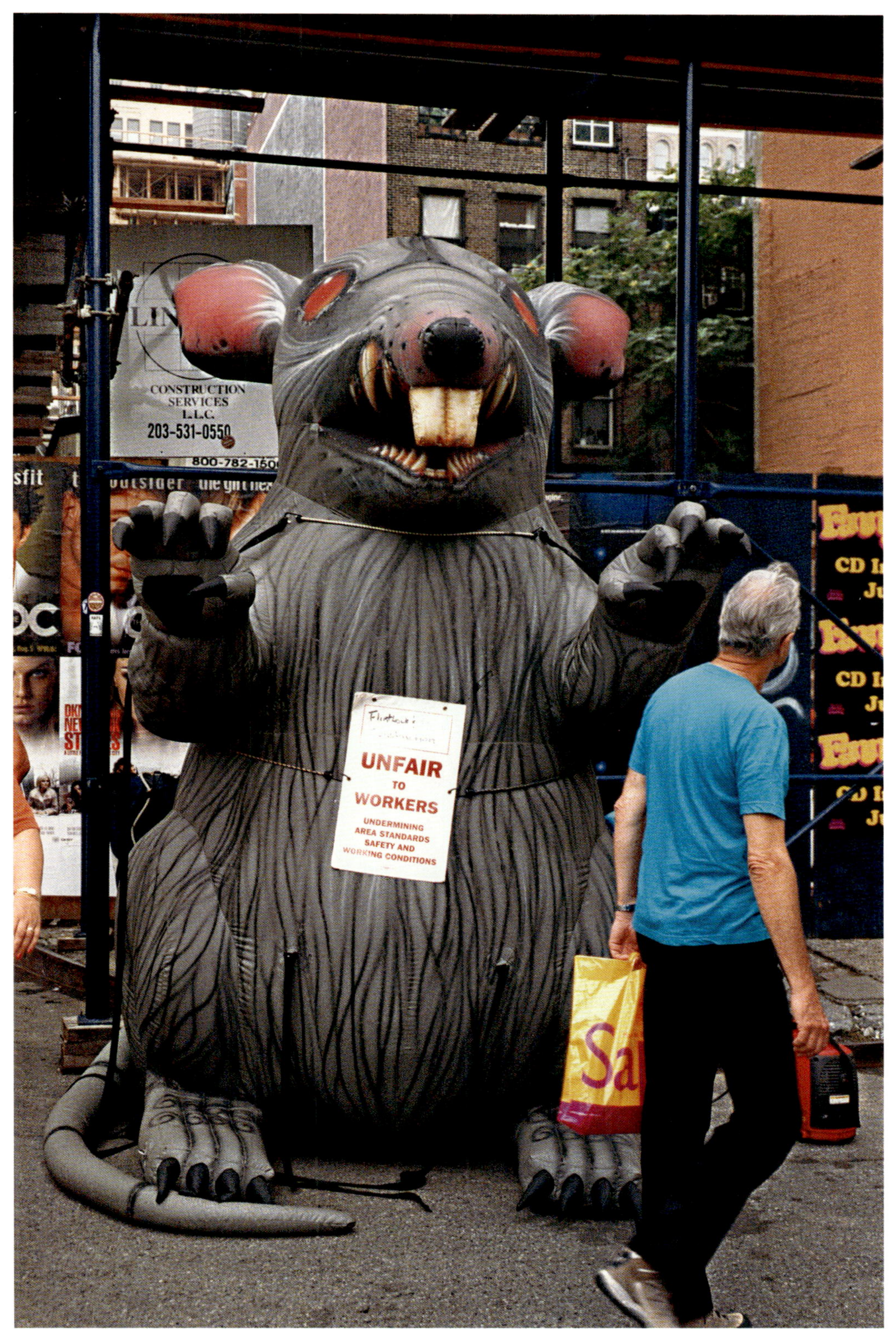

Unfair to Workers, New York, 2004

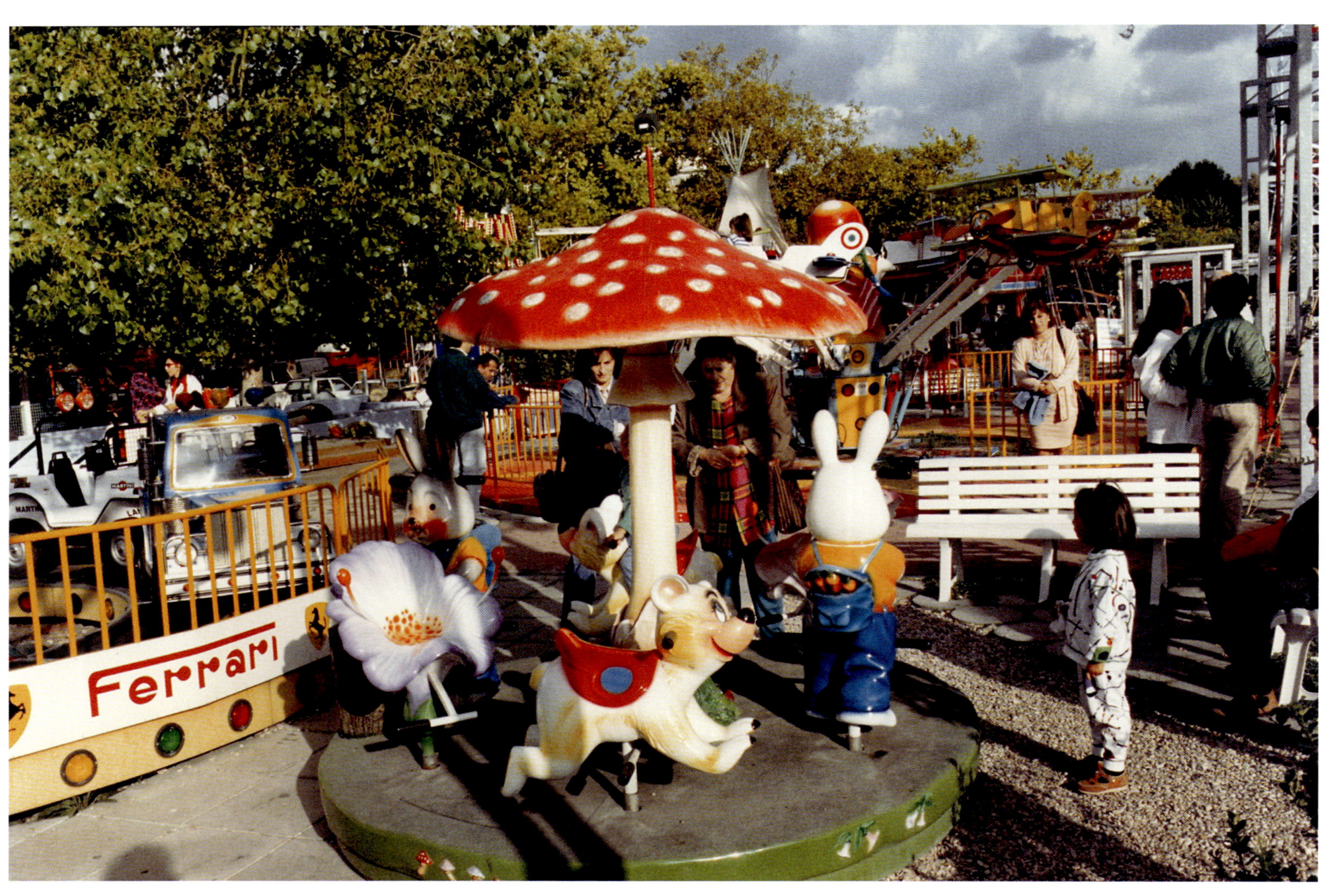

Kiddy Park, Ostia Antica, Italy, 1983

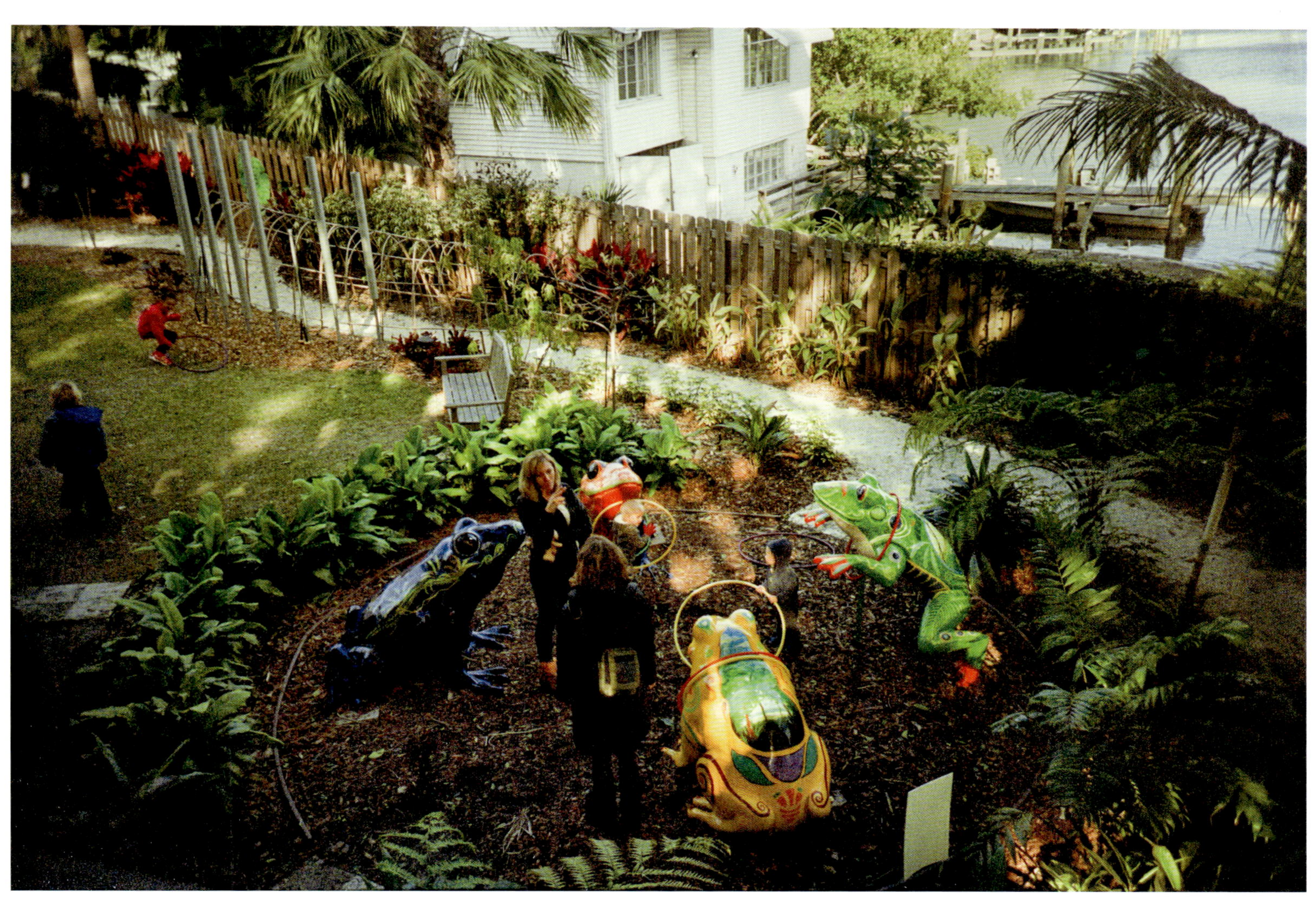

Meeting With Larger than Usual Frogs, Sarasota Botanical Garden, 2017

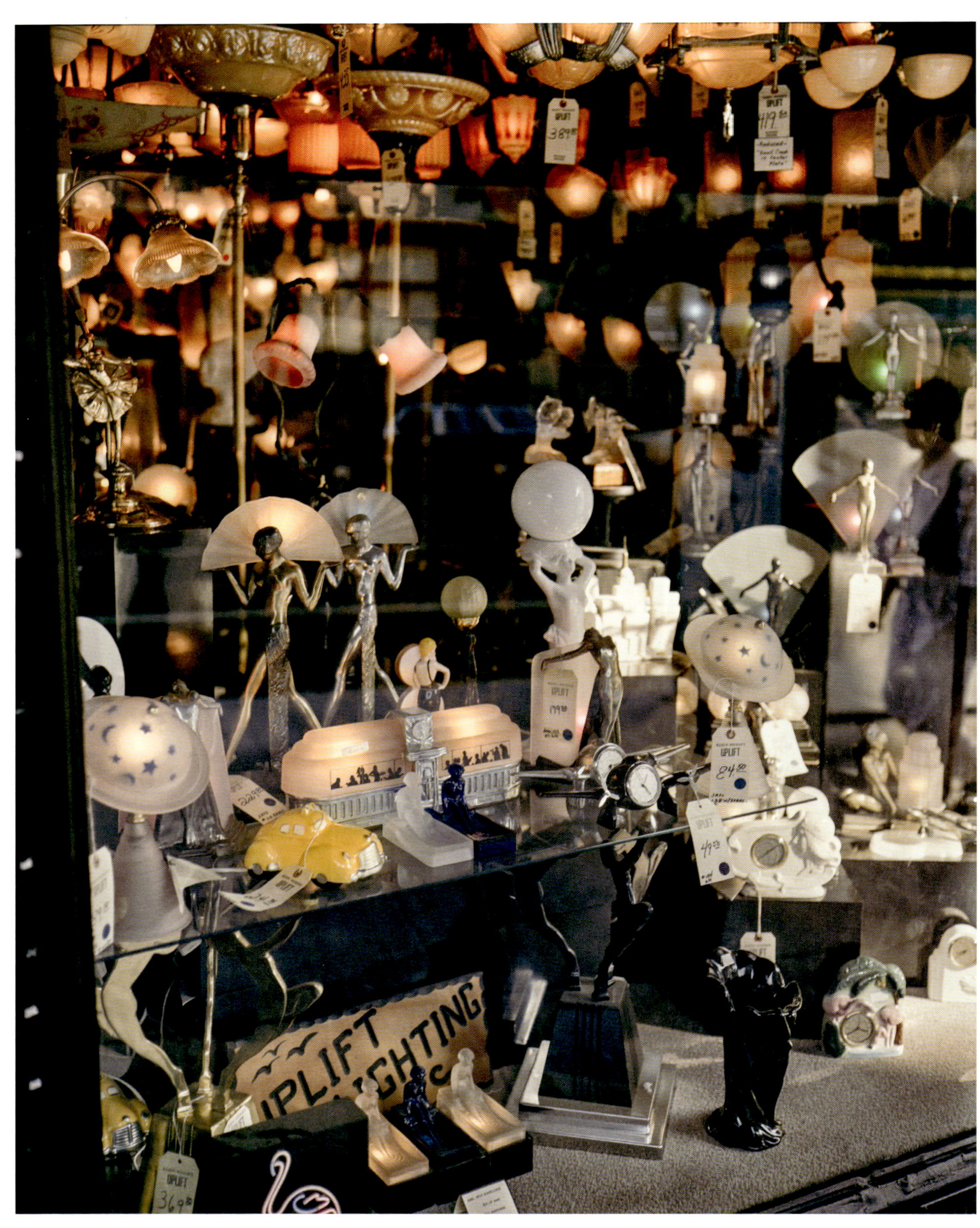

Novelty Shop Union Square, New York, date unknown

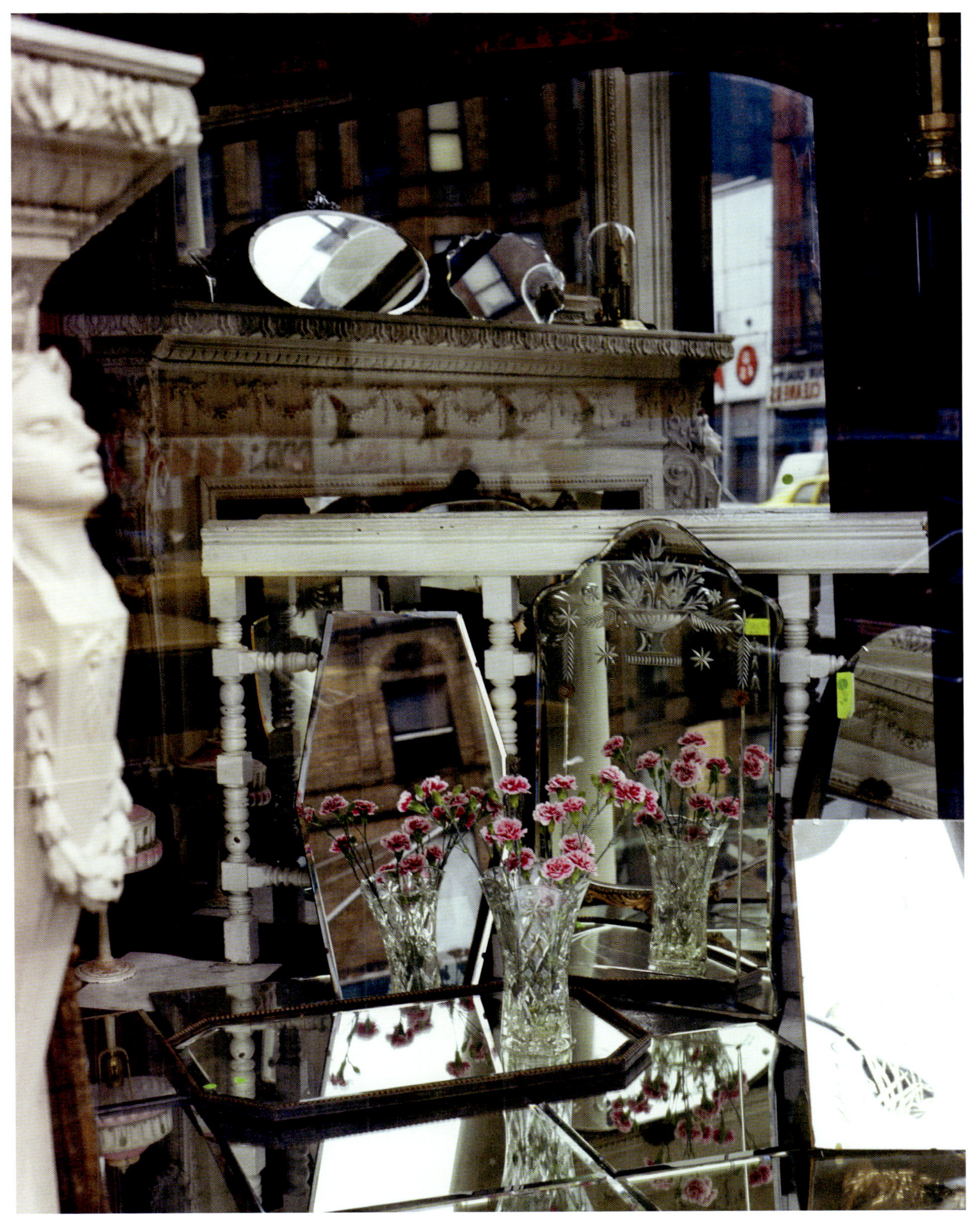

Cut Glass and Antique Mirrors, Columbus Ave., New York, 1979

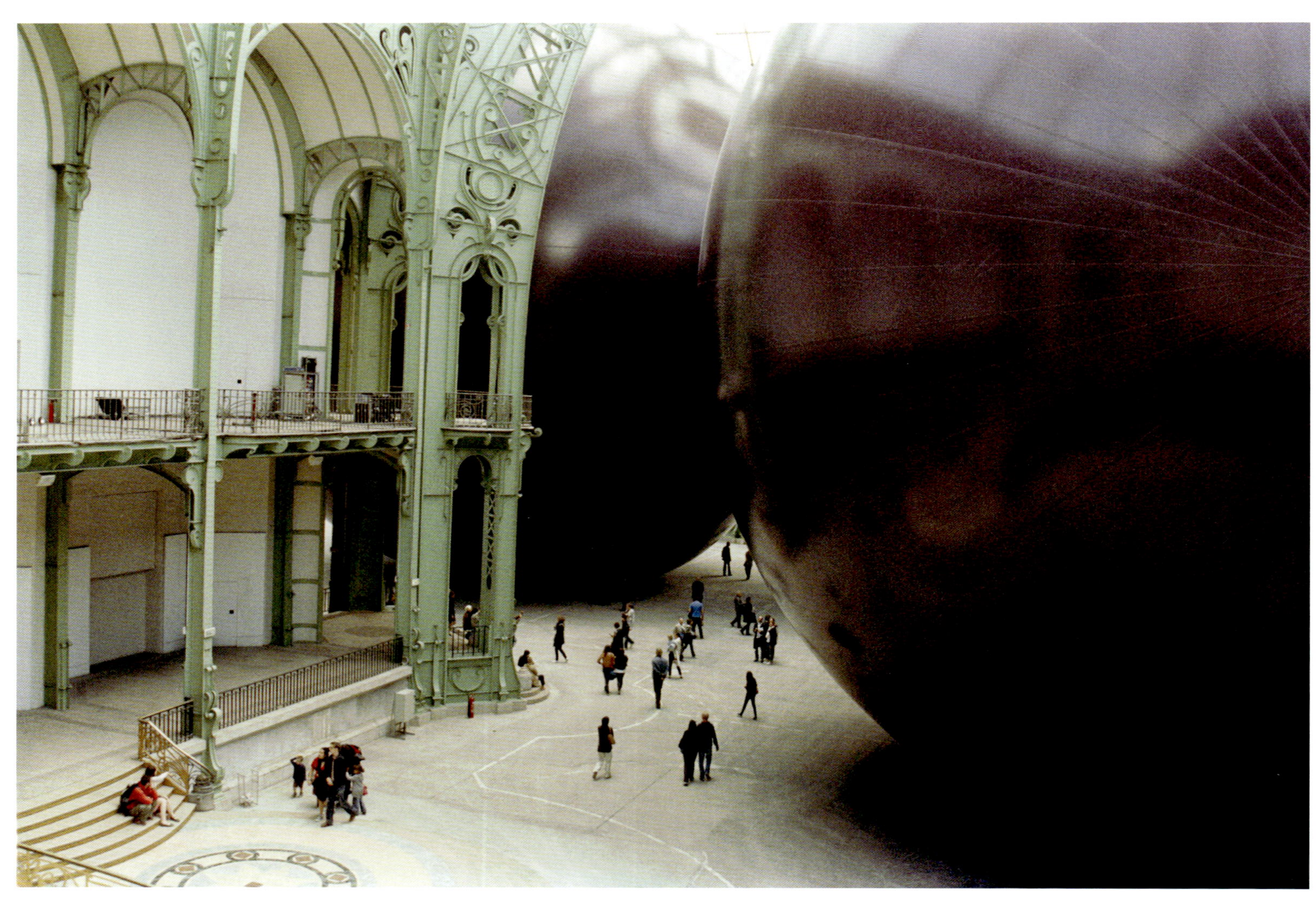

Large Sculpture by Anish Kapoor, Grand Palais, Paris, 2011

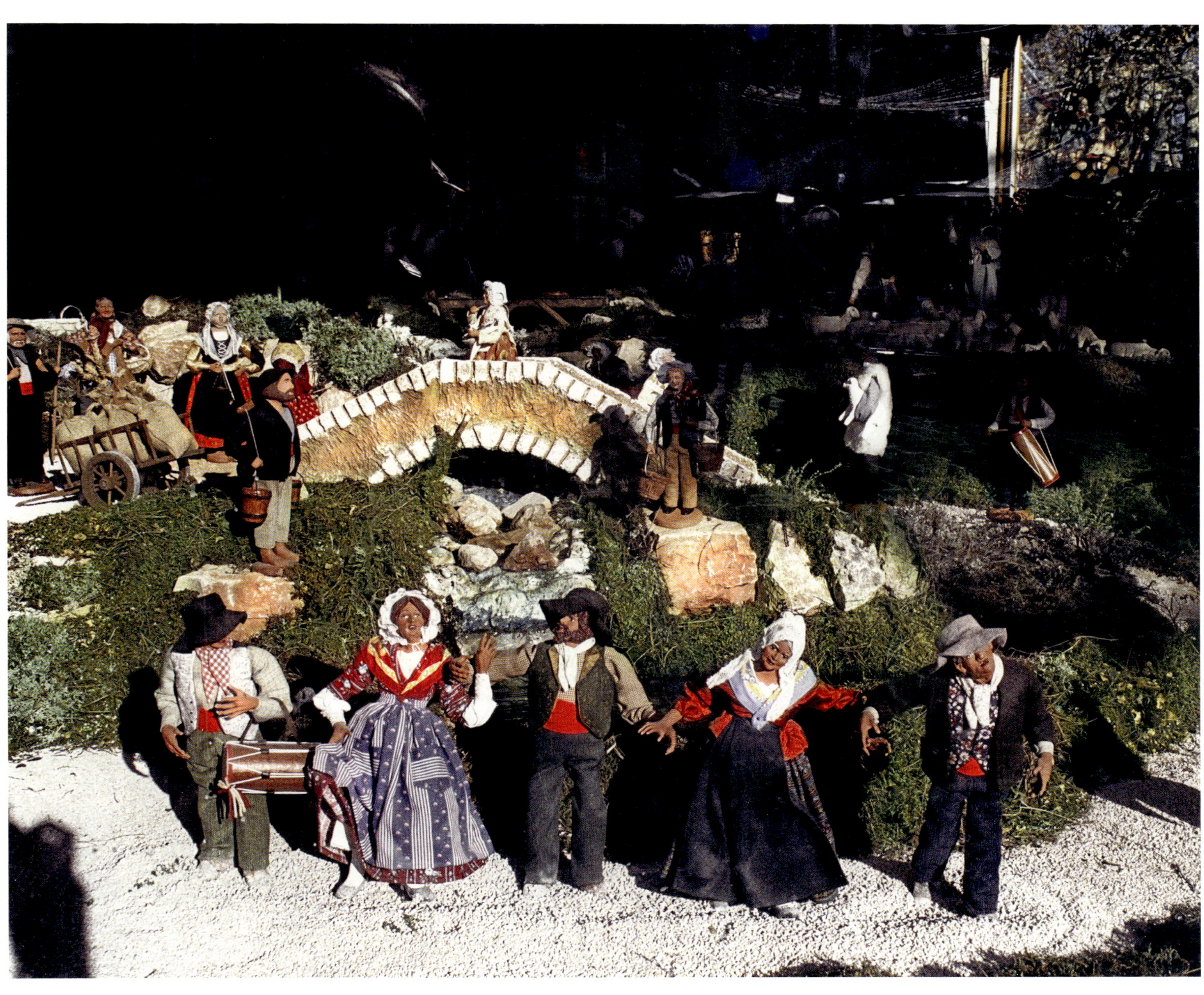

Santon Figures, Aubagne, France, 2004

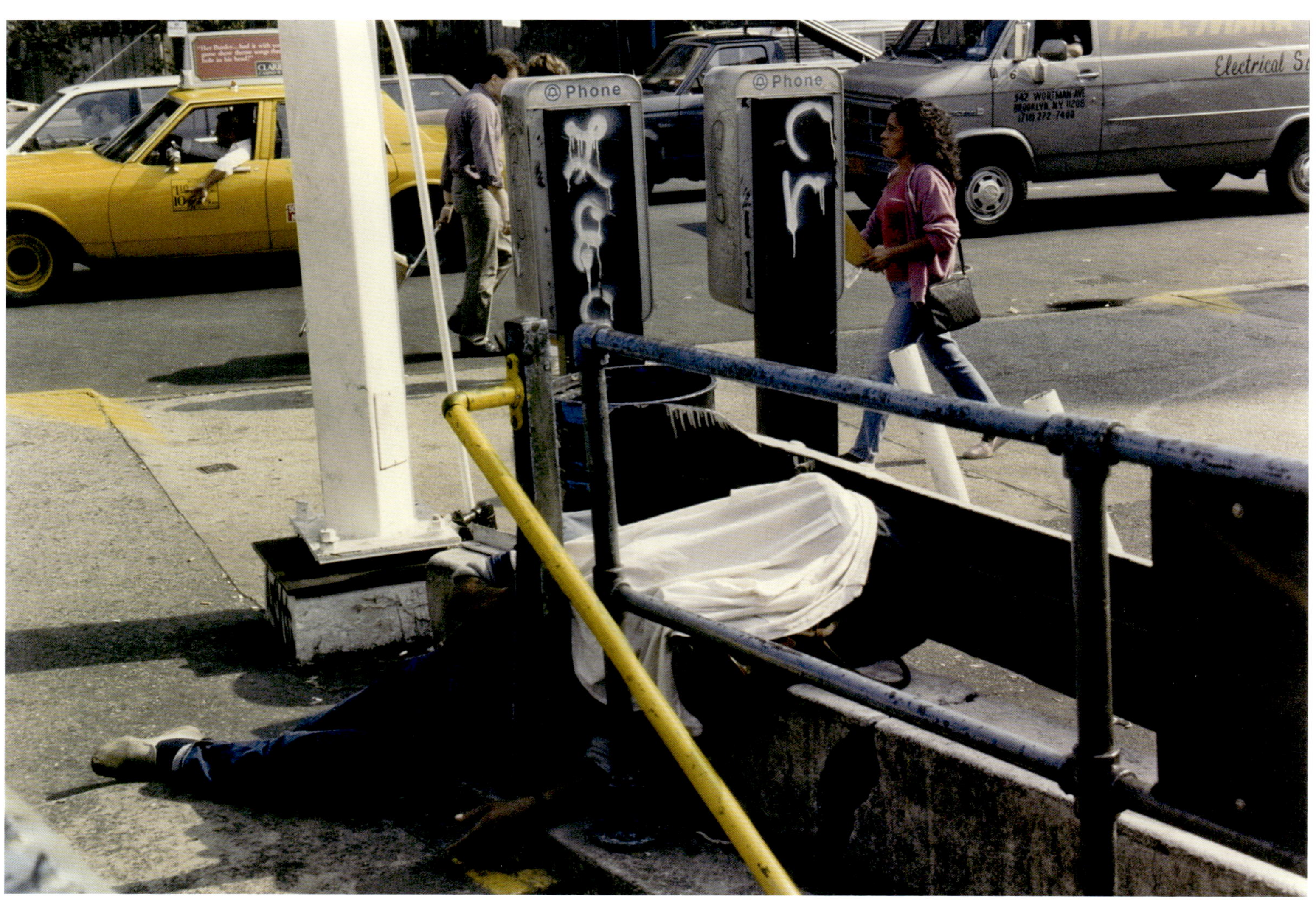

Recumbent Man, Subway Entrance, New York, 1985

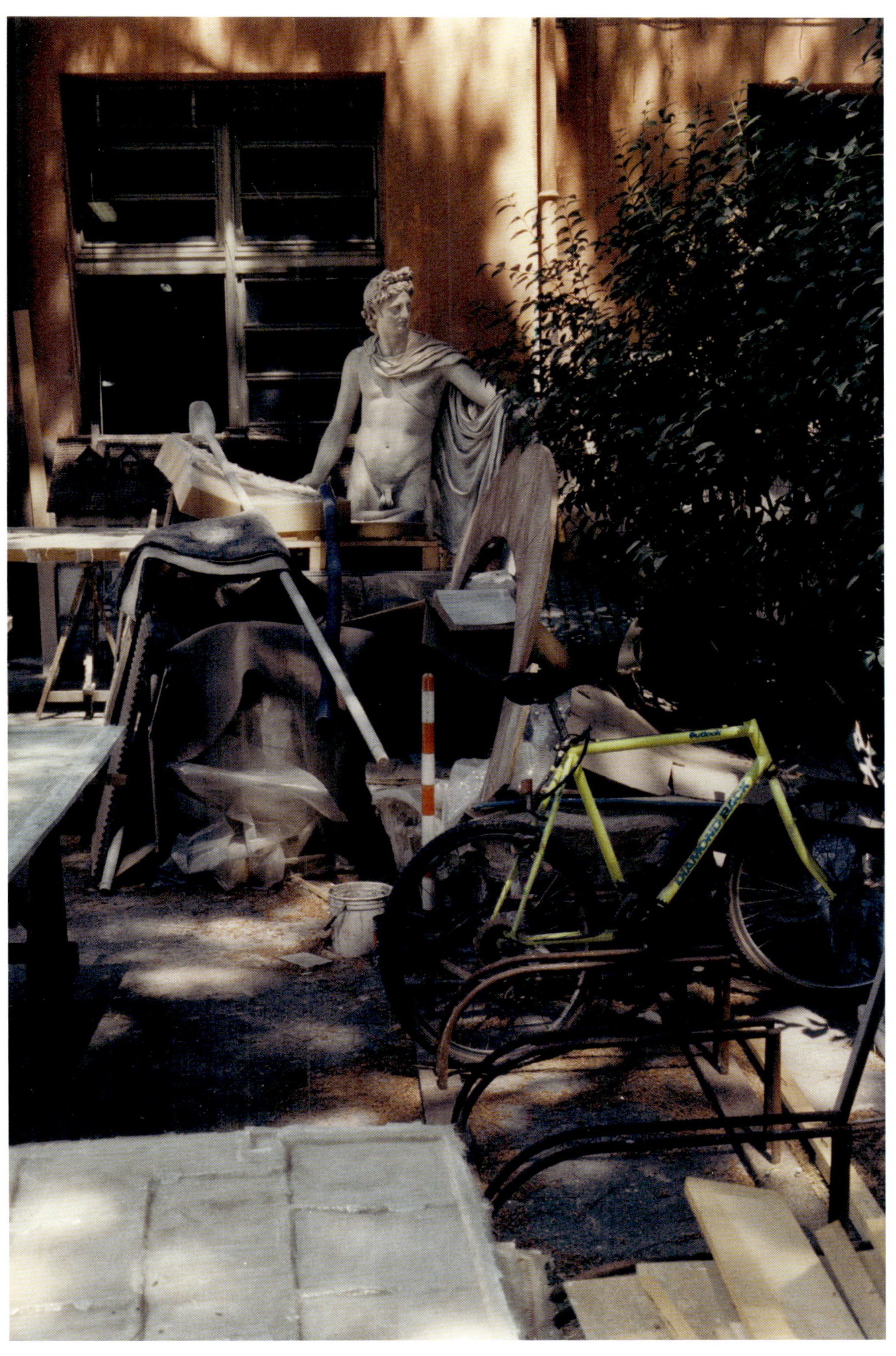

Studio Antiquities, Cinecittá Rome, 2000

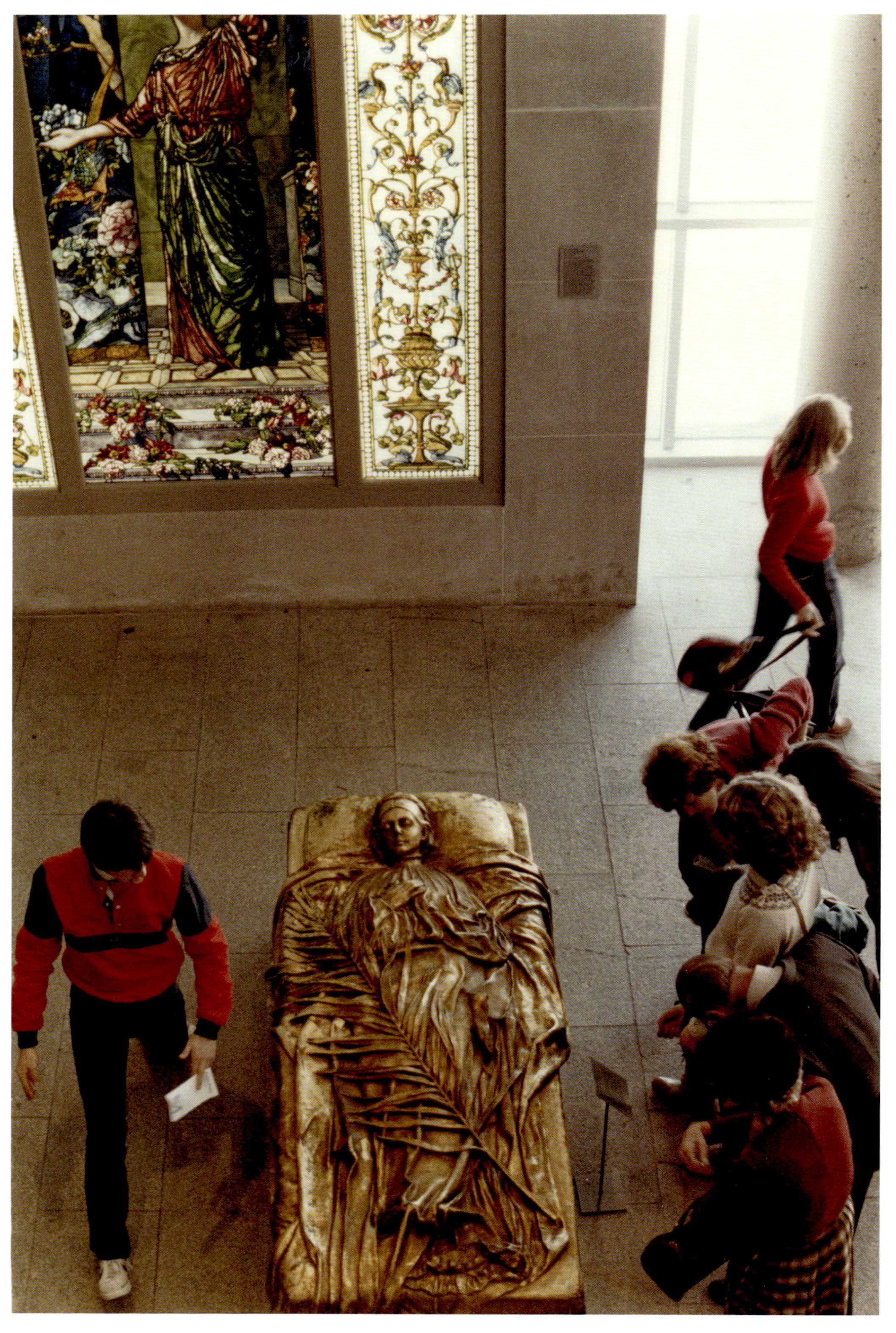

Memorial Tomb, Metropolitan Museum, New York, 1987

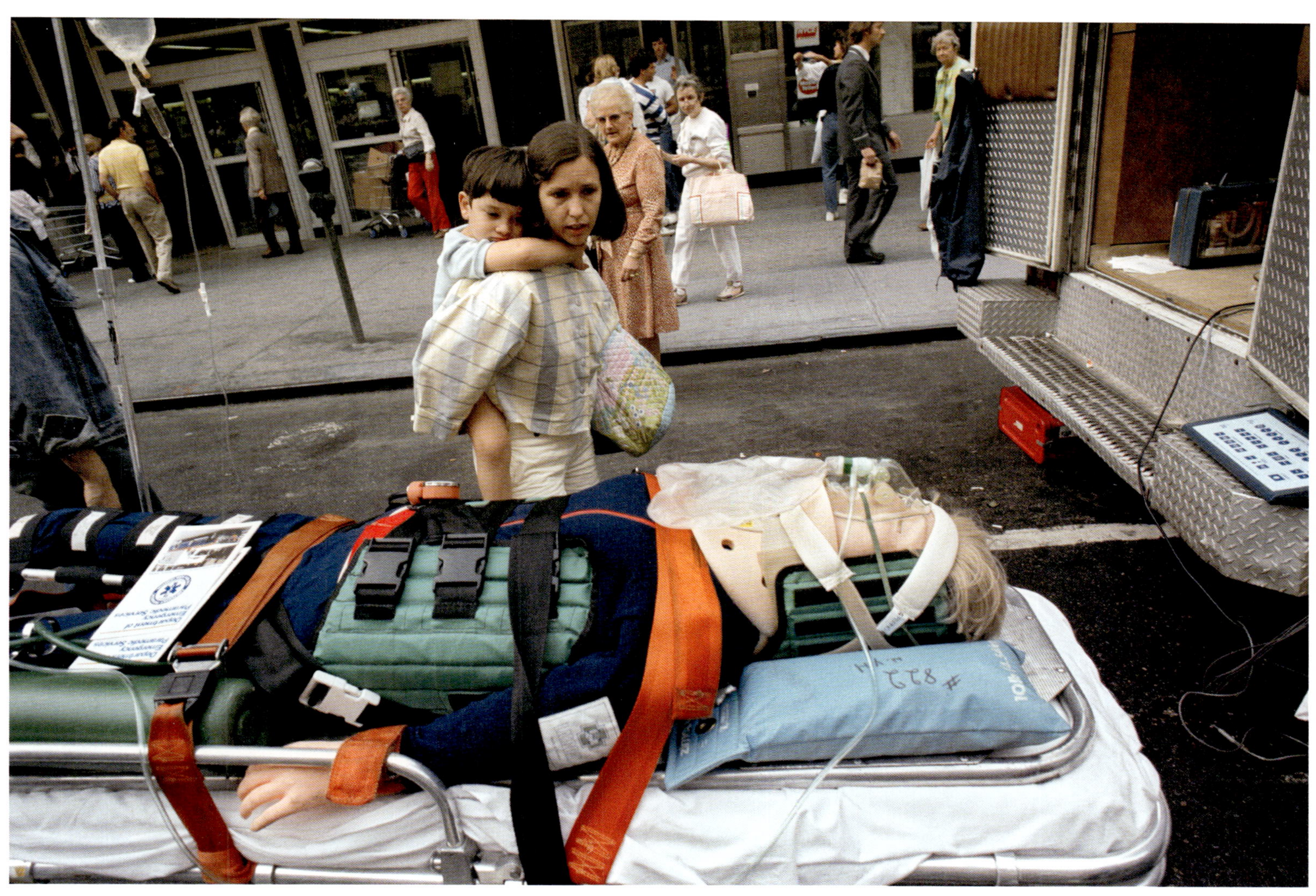

Simulated Emergency Victim, New York, 1998

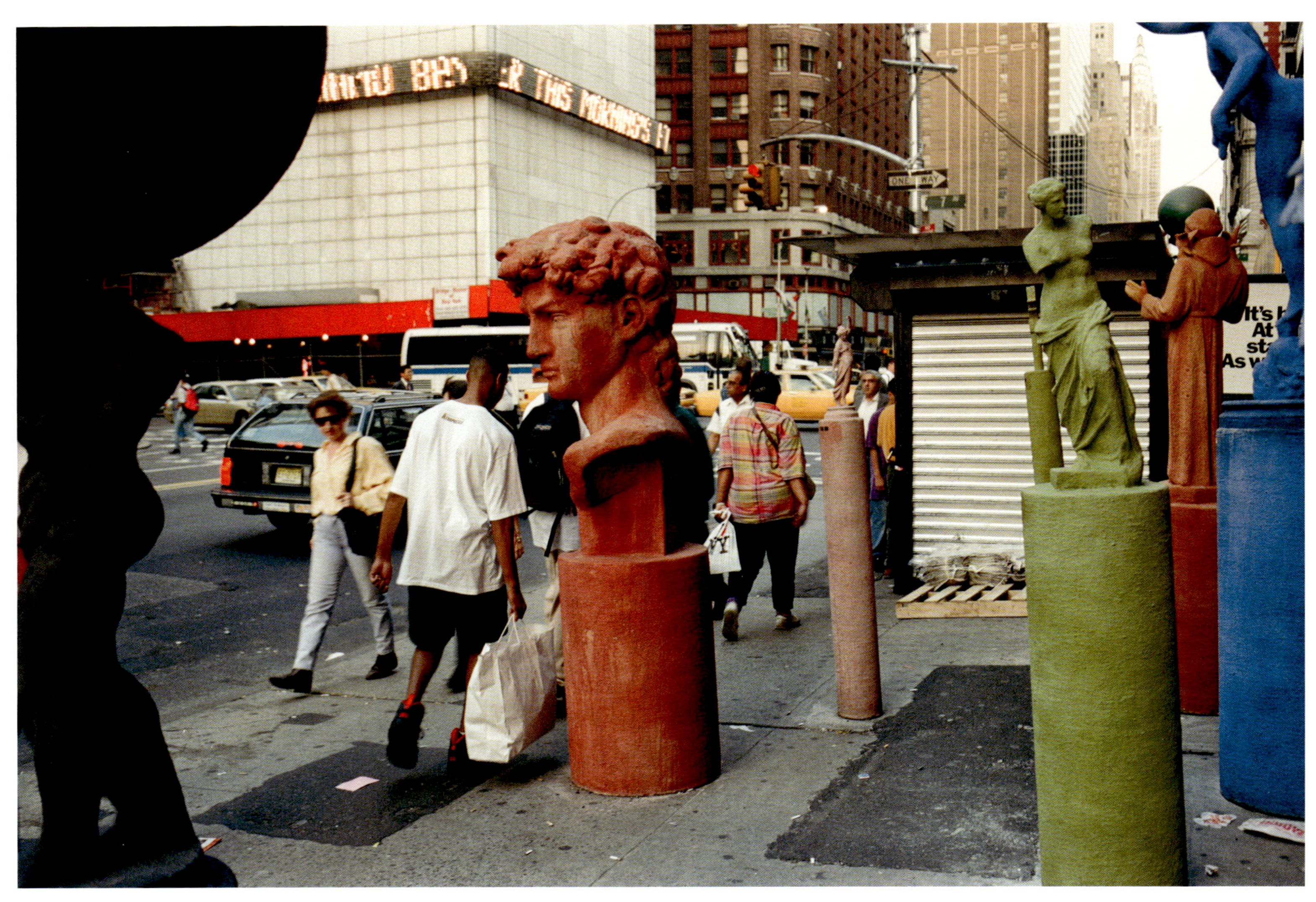

Reminiscence of Renaissance Sculpture by Ned Smyth near Times Square, New York, 1993

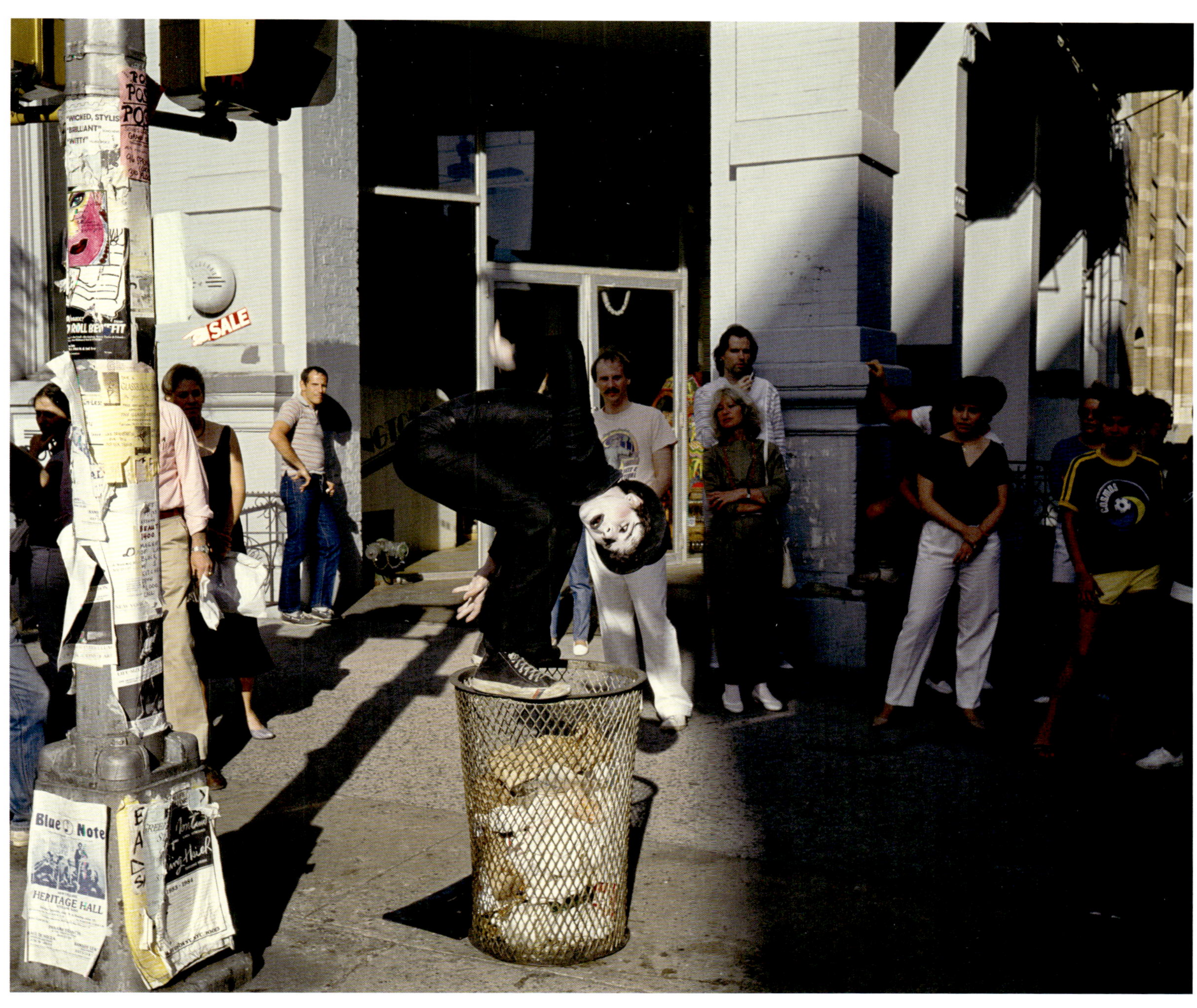

The Mime of Soho, New York, 1995

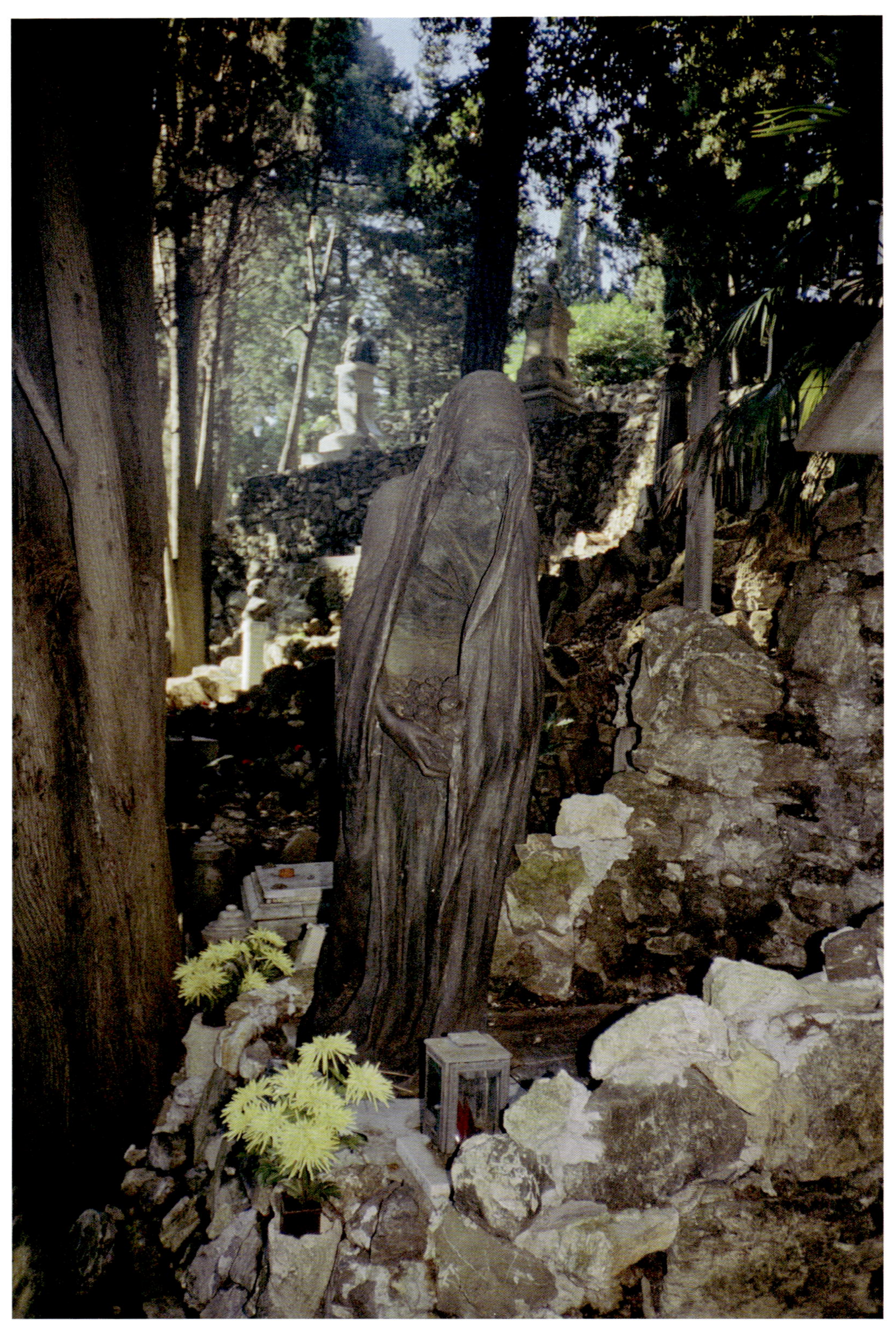

Mourning Figure, Staglieno Cemetery, Genoa, 2001

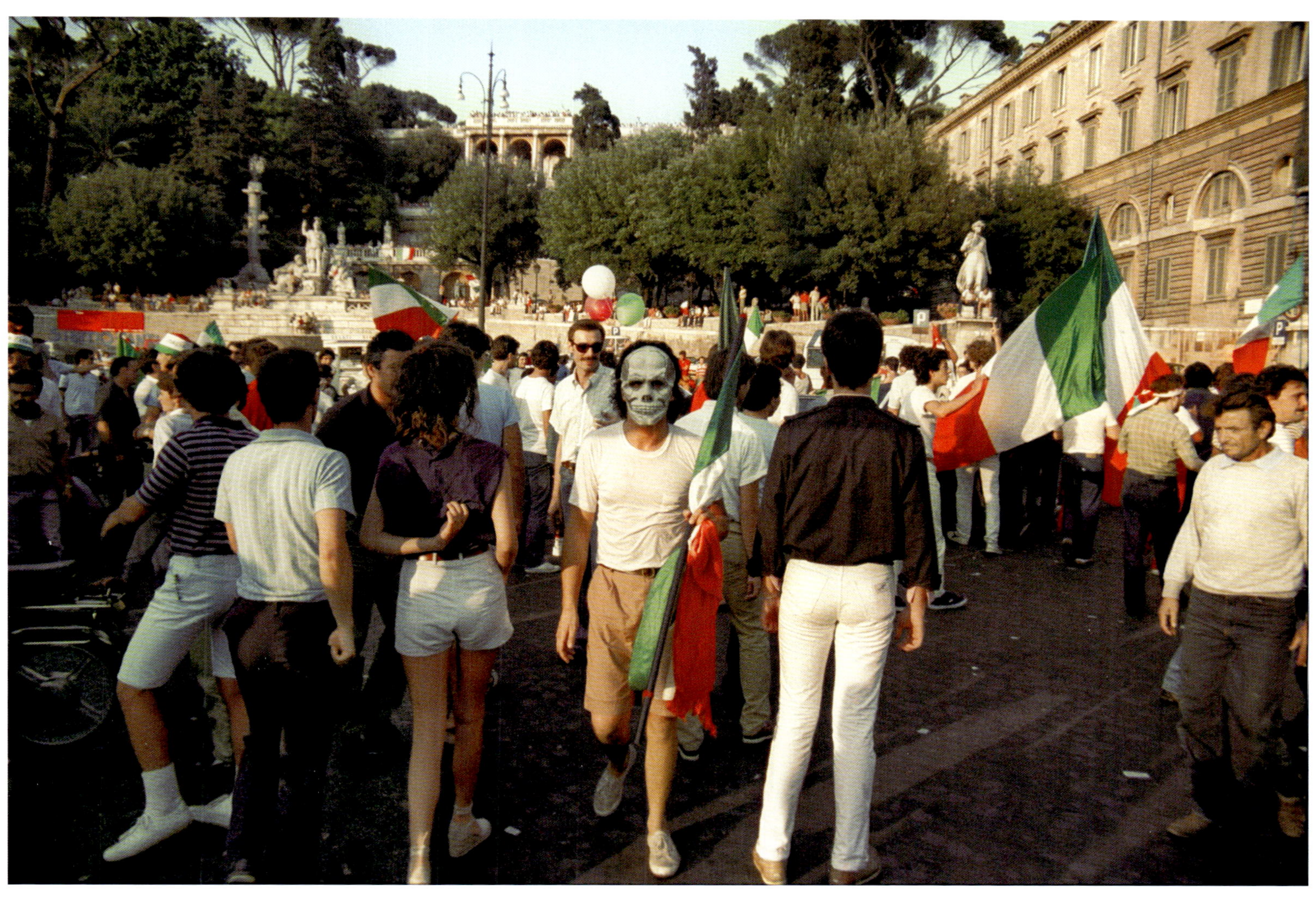

Spoiler, Soccer World Championship, Piazza del Popolo, Rome, 1982

ACKNOWLEDGMENTS

Among the people who helped make this book a reality, I celebrate the constructive work of my assistant Emily Kiacz. Not only did she make realistic suggestions, but she also contributed to the tactical underlying structure and themes of the book. Additionally, I want to thank and recognize Francesca Richer for her beautiful design. Lastly, I want to mention the support and affection of my wife Joyce in the furthering of this project's goals.

Published in the United States by powerHouse Books,
a division of powerHouse Cultural Entertainment, Inc.
32 Adams Street, Brooklyn, NY 11201-1021
e-mail: info@powerHouseBooks.com
website: www.powerHouseBooks.com

First edition, 2021

Library of Congress Control Number: 2020949895

ISBN 978-1-57687-964-1

Designed by Francesca Richer
Printing and binding by EBS Editoriale Bortolazzi, Verona

10 9 8 7 6 5 4 3 2 1

Printed in Italy